Becoming Remarkably Able

Becoming Remarkably Able

Walking the Path to Talents, Interests, and Personal Growth

For Individuals with Autism Spectrum Disorders and Related Disabilities

Jackie Marquette, Ph.D.

Foreword by Ann Turnbull

APC

Autism Asperger Publishing Co.
P.O. Box 23173
Shawnee Mission, Kansas 66283-0173
www.asperger.net

© 2007 Autism Asperger Publishing Co.
P.O. Box 23173
Shawnee Mission, Kansas 66283-0173
www.asperger.net • 913.897.1004

Publisher's Cataloging-in-Publication

Marquette, Jackie.
    Becoming remarkably able : walking the path to gifts, interests, and personal growth for individuals with autism spectrum disorders and related disabilities / by Jackie Marquette; foreward by Ann Turnbull. — 1st ed.— Shawnee Mission, Kan. : Autism Asperger Pub. Co., 2007.

       p. ; cm.

       ISBN: 978-1-934575-01-7
       LCCN: 2007932564

       Includes bibliographical references.
       Audience: parents, counselors, and young adults with autism spectrum disorder and other related disabilities.
       "Walking the Path (WP) is a practical model for youth with ASD and developmental disabilities (DD) who are in transition from adolescence to adulthood."--Intro.

       1. Developmentally disabled children--Handbooks, manuals, etc. 2. Autism--Handbooks, manuals, etc. 3. Developmentally disabled children--Treatment. 4. Autism--Treatment. I. Turnbull, Ann. I. Title. II. Becoming remarkably able : walking the path to gifts, interests, and personal growth for individuals with autism spectrum disorders and related disabilities.

RJ506.A9 .M37 2007
618.92/8588--dc22

0708

Cover by Trent Altman, artist. To see Trent's art, log onto: www.independencebound.com/trentsprints

This book is designed in Futura and Trebuchet.

Printed in the United States of America.

Dedication

I dedicate this poem, personal story, and workbook to my son Trent and to people of all ages who live with daily challenges due to their disability or society's lack of awareness. Trent — through efforts, struggles, and accomplishments — is my inspiration. May young adults find meaning in daily living, courage to pursue a purposeful life, and a hand reaching out to help develop their skills and gifts.

Colors of Your Song

I see and feel all the colors of Your song.
Brilliant shades dance with my brush.
With each tint and blush I paint, I hear Your melody.

Words are not my way,
Conversation is not my forte.
But You are the One who knows me well.

I don't worry though,
the dazzling colors painted on
my canvas are my gifts to all.

Acknowledgments

I want to thank Ralph, my incredible husband, who first gave me the idea to write this workbook. Although there were some financial risks, he gave me the time and steadfast support to write. I am eternally grateful for his willingness to sustain me in every way.

I thank Ann Turnbull for writing the foreword. She has been a mentor to me throughout the years with her research in the area of family and community living.

I am sincerely grateful to Dr. Barry Prizant for writing a testimonial and taking time out of a full schedule to review my manuscript, make suggestions, and then recommend it for publication to the Autism Asperger Publishing Company.

I appreciatea John Kemp's testimonial, as he saw the book's message as being improtant to other groups of disability outside of autism.

I thank Kirsten McBride for all of her editing and questions that made the manuscript much clearer and focused. I also thank all the staff at the Autism Asperger Publishing Company.

I am grateful to Joe Paul Pruitt, my friend and editor of Harmony House Publishing, who has a strong sensitivity to understanding human life. His input has been invaluable.

I thank Dr. Steve Miller for editing early drafts of this manuscript before it was a book.

I want to thank all the students with special needs I have worked with throughout my career. They taught me the questions to ask that led me to new ways of perceiving and thinking about their needs and strengths.

I want to thank John Roberts, special education director of Hardin County Schools, Kentucky, for his leadership and openness to innovative employment projects that benefit students with special needs.

I thank my colleagues in Hardin County Schools. I especially thank Betty Horton and Donna Turner, who worked with me as a team to find good job matches for our students during my four years as a transition consultant. They are my friends forever.

I am grateful for Milton Tyree. I highly value his training through the Community Based Work Transition Program. I learned from him how to recognize the gifts that people with disabilities offer in the area of employment. I also appreciate him for participating in Trent's person-centered planning meetings.

I thank Denny Simonavice, the manager at Meijer, INC. where Trent works, and all of his co-workers, who show a willingness to offer natural supports to Trent.

I am sincerely grateful for the Supported Living grant that has opened numerous doors to the community for Trent.

I am grateful for Barry Whaley and Troy Klabor at Community Employment who have shown a genuine interest in Trent, helping him get jobs at Kmart and Meijer. I sincerely appreciate all their ideas and actions, along with their participation on Trent's person-centered planning meetings.

I send my thanks to every mom who sent me emails of continual support for my work and expressions of their hopes and desires for their child to walk the path to community living.

I thank Jason Williams, Trent's housemate and "domestic advisor," as he always humorously comments. He continues to willingly guide and encourage Trent to give his best at work and in various community settings. He is truly a member of our family.

I give thanks to my mother for her delight in my accomplishments and her joy in Trent's.

Finally, I give my thanks to my three sons — Todd, Trent, and Travis — for bringing a joy to my life that soars beyond words.

— J M

Foreword

After reading *Becoming Remarkably Able*, I had flashbacks of our family's own transition 17 years ago when JT, our 37-year old son who has cognitive and mental health challenges, was transitioning from high school to adulthood. We could have surely used this workbook at that time. The major challenge was that the services and supports in our community that were available were not consistent with JT's values, strengths, preferences, and needs, nor of ours. The available path was not the right one for JT and our family. And the last thing that we wanted to do was to start yet another community program that would, indeed, reflect our values. Our decision was to embark on the path in terms of trying to improve the existing available services and supports which resulted in a very frustrating and unsatisfactory experience for everyone. In other words, it was a path that resulted in JT becoming "remarkably DISabled." I will always recall the advice given to us by a family friend at that time, "Ann and Rud, no matter how far down the wrong path you go, if it's the wrong path, turn around." We did turn around, and I'm delighted to say that 17 years later JT and our family are on the path to independence and, yes, to BEYOND.

As I reflect, oh, how easier it would have been if we had had Jackie's workbook. What strikes me most about this workbook is that the contents of it are as vibrant and energizing as its striking and beautiful cover. Trent, Jackie's son with autism, created the compelling portrait of "the path" on the cover. Jackie, with her remarkable parental insights, filled the contents with a decision-making approach to self-determination that I would describe as relationship-based, hopeful, constructive, action-oriented, individualized, and reflective. It puts families, individuals with disabilities, and their reliable allies in the "driver's seat" of decision-making in tailoring adult futures for the individual and for the family that are wholly consistent with what will make their "chimes ring." Because every single family and every single individual with a disability is unique, this workbook builds on that uniqueness by guiding people through a *process* of reflection and interactive planning.

If our family had had this workbook 20 years ago and had followed its process, our path would not have been as bumpy; and we would not have had to turn around, but rather we would have started on the right path.

I highly recommend *Becoming Remarkably Able: Walking the Path to Independence and Beyond*. From my own professional and family experiences, this, indeed, is a *remarkable* resource.

Ann Turnbull,
Co-Director, Beach Center on Disability
Professor, Department of Special Education
University of Kansas
"Veteran" of adult transition

*"And the day came when the risk it took
to remain tight inside the bud
was more painful than the risk
it took to blossom."*

Anais Nin

Table of Contents

Introduction

Sitting in a bookstore cafe on a rainy afternoon, I read a quote by Theodore Roethke, "I learn by going where I have to go." That phrase describes the direction I chose to take 25 years ago. That "path" led me to solutions to help my son Trent eventually live an adult life with meaning and purpose.

Trent was diagnosed with autism at the age of 3. After asking many questions and searching for answers, I decided to move ahead with the conviction that he would reach a full, happy, and independent life as an adult, despite having autism. There isn't anything in the Walking the Path model in this book that I haven't questioned, tested, retested, studied, tried professionally and, equally important, initiated personally with my son. The book is grounded in (a) quality-of-life research on people with disabilities within the past 23 years, (b) tools and strategies I learned through trial and error and approaches other students and families have used, and (c) findings from my own research of 15 young adults with an autism spectrum disorder (ASD), who achieved independent living, employment, and enjoyment and acceptance in activities with people with whom they feel safe and accepted.

Walking the Path (WP) is a practical model for youth with ASD and developmental disabilities (DD) who are in transition from adolescence to adulthood. It is a creative, action-oriented process to discover a student's strengths and gifts. With supports, it will lead the student to employment, leisure, and greater community independence.

Perhaps you are a parent, advocate, or professional:

- concerned about the quality of a student's adolescent or adult years?

- seeking help to build a more meaningful life for a son/daughter?
- wanting to know how the young adult can enter integrative community settings and have opportunities to continue grow personally?
- desiring to learn what steps to take so the young adult can access employment, attend college, participate in leisure/hobby, or have more independence?
- curious about the future because you have a child or work with children diagnosed with autism or other severe disabilities?

If you are facing any of these issues or concerns, the WP will be helpful to you. The information presented here is based upon the following premises:

1. Each adolescent or young adult is special and can develop to his or her fullest potential.
2. Individuals with diverse levels of severity can benefit from the ideas and activities presented here to become more capable in all areas of living. Labels such as "high functioning" and "low functioning" are not the criteria to determine if the model is applicable. WP can help guide all individuals regardless of the disability severity. Labels serve no purpose here.
3. Every student or young adult has a viable gift, strength, and/or interest that may only need uncovering to blossom.
4. Supports or accommodations are necessary in order for a person to explore and identify strengths that will open different community settings.
5. We never stop learning and growing. Therefore, making progress in skill development and personal growth in adulthood is a not a myth, but a reality. Indeed, growth continues into adulthood.
6. "Independent living" refers to persons with a disability living at their highest capability level regardless of the "supports" that assist them in participating in everyday activities, such as having a job or living in an apartment or house. A person who reaches "independent living" may do so with few supports. Yet, a person can also live "independently" with all kinds of supports. Thus, "independent living" means *never* going it alone.

Youth see in themselves what we see in them. Each has the most basic right to enjoy continued growth, find happiness, and contribute something positive to the world. We are all essentially "advocates," to include the person with ASD or DD, family members, professionals, and the community. As all of us create a larger vision of a student's capabilities, the greater will be his willingness to act upon personal strengths and gifts that we *acknowledge* and *support*. In other words, a student with a disability will see how capable he can become through our eyes. My highest vision is that any person with any disability can deeply feel or say, "I belong; I matter; I am accepted."

Currently, there are few positive examples of people with severe disabilities living with purpose and independence in the community. In the midst of critical resource shortages, families with youth who have more involved disabilities are desperate for options. Information and governmental support programs that provide knowledge and the "how to" of establishing community living are often nonexistent. Many families see no other choice but to keep a young adult at home, in a day program, or in a sheltered workshop.

Disability list serves on the Internet make daily announcements of parental family struggles, crises, and tragic outcomes for children and adults who are either without resources and services or living isolated.

But there is good news. Parents and professionals are rallying together to demand and work toward community outcomes for youth other than the current options. Many parents are unwilling to accept isolation and/or day programs that limit the young adult's growth or fail to promote independence and well-being.

The WP Process

Walking the Path provides a process that includes all stakeholders in creating options that promote personal growth in youth and greater community participation. The process is multifaceted and multidimensional. It is not linear. You will no*t* find a consecutive, step-by-step approach. That is not possible with any creative process. You start with a blank slate and then you guide the adolescent/young adult into the exploratory process. You do not necessarily know what you will learn or discover. Surprising outcomes have occurred during this exploration, such as being referred to someone who will teach a particular skill, being offered a paid job with the support to learn tasks, joining an exercise club where a volunteer retired military officer will coach the young adult in developing strength and using the machines, or an upper-level college student guiding and supporting a freshman in her first semester of college.

Terms You Will Encounter in This Book

"Remarkably able" — a term I use to describe the individual who becomes involved in the process of exploring who he really is through opportunities to self-express. Remarkably able refers to the student/young adult's unique personal expression revealed through his specific gift, interest, or strength.

Initiating the first steps in this process can lift the individual to a higher level of self-awareness, self-expression, and capability. The act of exploring and identifying a gift is one thing, but to use and apply a recognized strength or gift can open a new world to peer connections, participation in organizations/clubs, leisure, suitable employment, defined career direction, and interpersonal growth with increased independence.

A gift — something a person is born with. It's something that comes as easily as breathing.

A talent — a gift the individual has pursued, developed, and refined.

A skill — something one learns to do. It may draw upon a person's gifts.

An interest — something that draws one's attention.

An experience — an emotional or mental perception that a person has or something physical that h/she has done (Gillman, 1997, p. 3).

Strengths — usually more voluntary than gifts and talents. Possessing a strength involves choices about when to use it and whether to keep building upon it. For example, telling the cashier that he undercharged you $5.00 is personal strength and a decision to apply it. Thus, strengths can be built upon with time and effort (Seligman, 2005).

Value — something of substance and/or merit; has a connection with a person's strengths.

About Supports

To increase successful student transition outcomes, we must design and create "supports" that enable the individual to reach a higher level of capability and personal growth. I define a "support" as any type of assistance — "technical," "device or equipment," "people support" or an opened, positive attitude — that elevates a person to do or become what she could not on his or her own. Although supports may look different for each person, they are necessary in order for the individual to step into areas where she can explore interests, practice and develop skills, use a gift, or participate in integrative opportunities with typical peers and among various community settings.

When various levels of support are in place, a range of outcomes can happen, from having a job and going to school, to accessing even the most basic elements of everyday living in the community. If outings have become rare for the adolescent/young adult, consider how precious just shopping at the grocery store becomes. The supports that contribute to being able to participate in this way may be as simple as the young adult having a check list to refer to and money in his wallet. For someone else, it may be having a "support person" drive her and walk with her through the grocery store to help read labels and signs and choose items to purchase. For a person with severe issues, the support person may redirect inappropriate behaviors and offer feedback on making choices as well.

About Independent Living Skills

Learning independent living skills is significant in a student's preparation for community adaptation. However, learning and applying these skills is only a small part of the person's overall capability for success and a fulfilling life.

Learning about self-awareness, advocating for one's needs, and applying constructive responses and actions is all part of handling daily challenges and adapting among ever-changing life conditions. In this regard, a domain that is critical is emotional strength. For example, it takes emotional strength to stay at school or on the job until the end of the school day or the shift even when one is slightly ill. Unfortunately, instruction and supports that build emotional strengths are missing from research-based independent living models as well as services and programs for youth with disabilities.

Current delivery of community living services suffers from two major problems. First, the requirement to achieve "independent living skills" often excludes individuals who need more support to learn and adapt to the community. These persons may have labels ranging from moderate to severely disabled. Second, individuals who are high-functioning and exhibit strong "independent living skills" capable of physical self-care, working a job, and paying bills are often limited emotionally and socially. Many lack the necessary supports to take positive steps to have a friend and to accept and move through loss, crises, rejection, daily setbacks, and loneliness.

Practices that push standards for individuals with disabilities to acquire a set of "independent living skills" *before* entering independent living are not valid. It is true that learning such skills is necessary, but these skills are only a part of the complete picture. As a person's interests are pursued and supports are in place to enable him to join and learn in new settings and with different peers, a higher capability, increased adaptation, and often a new personal profile is activated.

Much of the information in this book is based on results of my own research. Specifically, I conducted an in-depth qualitative research study whereby I interviewed 20 parents who had young adults with autism and who had guided them to independent living. Further, I developed the Capability and Independence Scale (CAIS), an assessment and planning tool designed to evaluate and guide adolescents and young adults to become more capable and more independent, and reach a life that reflects their needs and own choices. The research provided strong validation for the scale and, most important, showed that the level of a person's adaptation and capability is not completely determined by his or her diagnosis and cannot be predicted by the severity of autism.

There is a great need for measurements that evaluate preparedness, support, and adaptation to all areas of community living. Indeed, there is a need to provide support for all youth, regardless of disability severity, that builds emotional growth for community adaptation. The WP model offers many options to supporting and to building emotional growth in individuals with ASD and DD.

Several areas related to creating independent living are not addressed in this book such as applying for a job, completing an application, interviewing tips, writing a business plan for self-employment, behavioral management strategies, accessing governmental resources, guardianship, trusts, wills, or financial planning. While these areas are important and need to be addressed, they are beyond the scope of this book. Besides, numerous books and other resources focus on these tasks and do it well.

All parents hope for the best for their children as they enter adolescence and adulthood. Often when receiving their child's early diagnosis, parents fear the unknown in the years ahead. Despite this fear, the parents in my study who had guided their children to independent living had an early positive belief for their sons and daughters to live their lives among others in the community. Indeed, all of them could see their child maturing and living his or her life valued for a unique contribution, however large or small. Each family formed a vision during their child's earliest years that became the foundation for thousands of actions related to development of individual education programs (IEP), therapy, and learning approaches, but also important recognizing the strengths and gifts that were innate in their child. Families became empowered and driven to assist their young adult as they proceeded through the steps. Thus, independent living was created and supported from the vantage point of the person's interests with supports to develop strengths and gifts.

This book is my gift to you, offering you what other parents and I have learned. Developing a vision for our child to have his unique life is work, yet it is an option and a choice. When options are so limited, youth and families need to hear every option available in order to make sound choices. This book is one. The pyramid illustrates the levels of action and supports that enable higher personal growth and capability in individuals with ASD and DD.

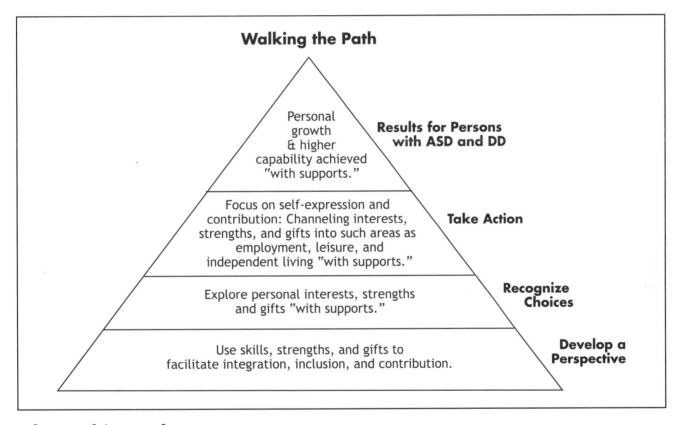

About This Book

The WP workbook contains five chapters. **Chapter One: Blazing a Trail** provides information from research on topics that ground the ideas and concepts presented in this book. The format includes questions and answers drawn from research. **Chapter Two: Role of the Professional** considers the role of professionals in guiding youth through transition as well as collaborating with families. **Chapter Three: Role of the Family,** writing from one parent to another, establishes a vision with goals that promote both the young adult's growth and the family's. **Chapter Four: Young Adult Roles** contains activities to help youth identify their strengths, gifts, and interests by writing a Gifts and Talents Action Plan (GTAP). **Chapter Five: Walking the Path Model — Purposes and Advantages** discusses the overall benefits of the WP model and offers conclusions.

The book also includes seven appendices. As you approach and work through activities for an individual or for yourself, frequently refer to these appendices, which offer extensive lists of gifts and strengths, supports that can be negotiated and created, ideas for community settings to access, state and governmental funding resources, and useful web sites and list serves.

It is my hope that the WP will:

- empower and heal families enough to envision a meaningful life for the child or young adult,
- gently nudge everyone out of a self-fulfilling doomsday mentality into a life of positive risk taking, and
- entice all advocates/professionals to consider new methods of service delivery.

"Accepted" and "respected" are two words that reflect the quality of a person's quality of life. Achieving a life where youth reach acceptance and respect in schools, neighborhoods, and community requires all of us to shift our thinking. Each individual has strengths, interests, and/or gifts that can be developed to lift him to higher capability and increased personal growth and independence. One of the most rewarding contributions we, the advocates, can offer is collaboration among groups to help youth create a life, walk their own path, and bravely seek their own unique treasures of becoming *remarkably able*.

Good luck and enjoy the process!

"Never doubt that a small group of dedicated people can make a difference. Indeed it is the only thing that ever has."
— Margaret Mead

CHAPTER ONE

BLAZING A TRAIL

To understand the path ahead of us, let's review briefly what was paved behind us. We often understand our current situation more fully when we see how we arrived. Over the past 30 years, young adults with developmental disabilities (DD), including autism spectrum disorders (ASD), have realized increased community access, to include supported employment and living within the community. Yet, although success has been noted for some, disbelief continues to exist regarding the contributions that persons with disabilities can offer to society. In addition, the demand for community assistance continues for tens of thousands of individuals, who are at home, often isolated, waiting for services that connect them to the community (Sullivan, 2001).

Where We Have Been

Since the mid 1970s children with disabilities have had the opportunity to receive free appropriate education and resources to meet their needs. Whether the educational services were good, or lacking in some way, the days of free appropriate services end after high school. Facing the post-high school years can be overwhelming and frightening for both the individual and the family. Preparation is essential. Many families are shocked when they find out community services for adults with ASD are not available. Essentially, families and children with a disability are pioneers blazing new paths.

Segregation was the prevailing theme in disability programs from the 1920s through the 1970s. Closed attitudes and institutionalization caused persons with disabilities to be excluded from society and deprived of opportunities that were available to people without disabilities (Berkowitz, 1996). Families often chose institutionalization because they were convinced by professionals that their child needed 24-hour care and was better off with his/ her "own kind" (Meyer, 1980), but many families expressed anger and guilt as a result of institutionalizing their child (Vitello & Soskin, 1985).

Thanks to the work and efforts of advocates, prevailing views have changed so that people with disabilities now have a right to live and work in the community. Innovators from the 1960s and 1970s helped us understand that labels of disability not only come from the medical profession but also from society. An earlier social systems perspective on "mental retardation" helps clarify the rejection that people with autism and other developmental disabilities confront during contemporary times. Sarason and Doris (1979) view the social system as follows:

> Mental retardation is not a "thing," not a set of characteristics inherent in an individual, but a concept that both describes and judges interactions of an individual, a social content, and the culturally determined values, traditions, and expectations that give shape and substance to the context at a particular time. (p. 17)

Another perspective offered by Gold (as cited in Mcloughlin, Garner, & Callahan, 1987) places responsibility on society to include the individual with a disability:

> Mental retardation refers to a level of functioning which requires from society significantly above average training procedures and superior assets in adaptive behavior on the part of society, manifested throughout the life of both society and the individual. (p. ix)

The current principles for integrating even individuals with severe disabilities into society were born from Gold's philosophy that actions by others in society are necessary to enable a person to participate in integrated environment. In addition, a powerful movement in vocational training in the 1970s was spearheaded by Lou Brown (cited in Mcloughlin et al., 1987), who developed a "criterion of ultimate functioning" and asserted that training for adults should take place in a setting where it would be used.

The movement to deinstitutionalize persons with DD paralleled the mainstreaming movement during the 1970s, which first allowed children with disabilities to enter school programs. These changing perspectives led to the passage of Public Law 94-142, the Education of All Handicapped Children Act. Early studies revealed that children with severe and profound disabilities could benefit from appropriate instructional programs. We can be grateful to advocates who argued for changes in educational policy. Because of their work and efforts, our children today are afforded the opportunity to enter our public school and receive services.

With the freedom and rights given to children with special needs in the late 1970s and early 1980s, high school graduation became a reality for many. Within the past decades, these students were among the first with a developmental disability to move entirely through the educational system to graduation. These students and their families were truly pioneers. Students with DD furthered their development and independence, gaining skills and access to the community far beyond what would have been possible without special education services.

But with graduation comes the reality of adult life. These same young adults with DD need assistance to find and maintain a job, to participate in community activities, and to negotiate the daily routines of life. Their needs don't end with the closure of school days. They continue to require supports in order to enter and participate in inclusive activities.

Without supports, the individual is left with few options to interact and participate in activities outside the home. Further, without the option to choose, families are faced with reassuming additional and/or full care for the young adult with DD. Ironically, the explosion in the number of individuals with DD completing high school (and the accompanying crisis in access to programs and resources) was brought about by the overwhelming success of P.L. 94-142.

Another major piece of legislation, the Individuals with Disabilities Education Act, IDEA 1990, gives students full participation in the planning and choice of goals during school, and thereby a voice in planning their future. Thus, the individualized education program (IEP) must include a statement of transition when the student is 14 years old and no later than 16. It is important that parents know to ask for this service if it is not offered. The process during the high school years must actively involve the student's preferences for adult life in coursework. Thus, more than ever before, students with developmental disabilities are participating in building their own lives.

Transition and Quality of Life — Frequently Asked Questions

Below are some references extracted from the research literature about the transition of young adults with a developmental disability, community participation, and the family. This work grounds my recommendations, suggestions, and the activities for youth, parents, and educators/professionals presented in the last chapter. Knowledge is empowering. The more we know about what impacts lives, the better prepared we are to take progressive steps.

Can people with severe disabilities really live in the community?

No matter how severe the disability, all people belong in the community (Taylor, 1987). We must support people with disabilities to participate in community life. Advocates and policymakers must work together and commit to this alternative to restrictive settings or home environments. We must view the capability of individuals with a DD based on what they can do *with* support and assistance, *not* based on their limitations without support (Marquette & Miller, 2004).

Can people with disabilities continue to grow and learn past the age of 21?

Historically, it has been assumed that persons with various disabilities could not succeed in community settings or supported employment because no further growth could be expected beyond adulthood. As a result, community living services were not recommended. According to Greenspan and Wider (2006), however, the opposite is true: Limited growth for adults with developmental disabilities is more the result of restrictive special programs that offer limited opportunities for intellectual growth beyond the 10- to 12-year-old level. Thus, these programs often offer age-inappropriate activities and less than meaningful tasks that reinforce concrete thinking.

On the other hand, when youth have access to learning new skills within a particular setting (i.e., employment), adaptation is enhanced (Marquette, 2007). If it is recognized that restrictive environments can stagnate a person's growth, why not presume that engaging within the community at large into areas of interests *with supports* can enhance personal growth, thus, increasing the learning curve. Indeed, the evidence is here: There are individuals of all levels of disability (severe to high functioning) participating, growing, and maturing as adults and making successful adaptations.

What is the role of inclusive settings and language development?

Prizant and Wetherby (1998) report that children learn language best in the context of natural activities, events, and routines. Their approach encourages spontaneous and initiated language. Exposure to natural interactions within inclusive settings and opportunities is highly significant for learning. Although this research was intended to promote language, it has relevance far beyond — into continuous learning through integration within diverse community settings. Research in this area on adults is nonexistent.

What are family concerns about adolescents or young adults and independence?

Parents see their typical teenager leaving home after high school as a natural part of the family cycle. Yet, separation for the young adult with autism to live independently is a great concern for parents (Blue-Banning & Turnbull, 2002). Believing in the value of independence is one thing, but carrying it out is not easy when funding for programs is lacking and society often rejects families and their children with ASD and other disabilities. Parents become lost in the details of caring for the autistic child; all they see is the narrow, immediate picture — the problems, issues, and specifics of what needs to be done each day (Blue-Banning & Turnbull).

How is the family affected by the transition years?

Transition is about the student entering into post-high school life. These years significantly impact the family as well. Ferguson, Ferguson, and Jones (1988) examined family structure during the student's transition to adult life. They found three distinct changes during student transition: in the individual's status (school to agency); in the degree of a young adult's autonomy; and within the family.

Bureaucratic transition refers to the student's change from the school system to agencies that serve adults with developmental disabilities. This is often most difficult and confusing for families as the adult service system is completely different from the school system. Essentially, there are no guaranteed services. *Status transition* represents the change from childhood to adulthood. As the child enters adulthood it is natural that he or she desires autonomy. Families are often unaware of how to "let go" and allow or promote independence. The third change is the *internal family transition*. Change in family structure frequently produces overwhelming stress. Major life events such as divorce, death, loss of a job, and economic stress become more pronounced during the transition years. They are abrupt and change the family's daily functioning. This must be recognized when developing services and policies to meet the needs of families, whom the young adult often depends upon for guidance.

Why are sheltered programs considered outdated?

Some believe that individuals with severe disabilities cannot acquire the skills necessary for employment and, therefore, guide families to the unchallenging and less than meaningful activities of the sheltered workshop. With these limited perceptions, there is little motivation to create opportunities for persons with severe disabilities to enter integrated employment and community involvement. Mcloughlin, Garner, and Callahan (1987) refer to sheltered programs as the "safety net syndrome," because they are often the only option in the community for persons with severe disabilities.

Mcloughlin et al. encourage us to examine the question asked by many professionals and families, "Can all persons labeled developmentally disabled acquire the skills necessary to perform meaningful work successfully in integrated employment settings?" The concern here is "all." The authors challenge us to see that it is less harmful to believe "Yes, all can reach higher levels of capability with the proper supports and development of skills" than to say "No" and be wrong. "No" requires that we remain satisfied and accept the status quo. For individuals who have been called "implaceable," the challenge is to create job opportunities and supports that will allow these persons to have employment success.

What increases an individual's access into the community?

Accessing community settings in order to increase the individual's quality of life is often dependent upon the family being empowered to seek resources that help the young adult (Kosciulek, 1999).

What is "empowerment"?

There are as many definitions of "empowerment" as there are disagreements among experts regarding its meaning. For example, empowerment is defined as:

> the ability to access and control needed resources, make decisions, solve problems, and interact effectively with others to obtain needed resources. (Dunst, Trivette, Gordon, & Pletcher, 1989, p. 132)

Another definition of empowerment is offered by Stein (1997):

> The internal/psychological factors include a sense of control, competence, confidence, responsibility, participation, solidarity, and community. The situational/social aspects of empowerment include control over resources; interpersonal, work, and organizational

skills; decision-making powers; self-sufficiency; mobility; and "savvy" or an ability to "get around" in society. (pp. 256-258)

What is family empowerment?

One definition is as follows:

> Family empowerment constitutes examining patterns of family functioning, recognizing dysfunctional emotions and behaviors, acquiring insight about disability programs, developing political skills for negotiating bureaucratic agencies and regulations, accessing available resources, and initiating movement toward independent functioning for both the adult with the disability and the family. (Marquette & Miller, 2002, p. 15)

What limits a family's ability to become empowered?

It is significant to recognize what hinders people from becoming active and participating in their own lives. It takes support and courage to reach beyond what were familiar lifestyles in the past for people with disabilities. An individual or his/her family's empowerment is often decreased because of fatigue, less time for leisure activities, or negative reactions by society directed toward the individual or the family (Singer & Irvin, 1991).

I learned how significant empowerment is. It led me to see possibilities for Trent and myself. I sought examples of others who faced similar challenges and wanted to change the lives for their children with disabilities. These persons had found a way to reach their goals, and they offered me hope. I realized that when I released familiar, comfortable ways of functioning, such as not allowing Trent certain community experiences or not accepting a referral to assist Trent, I was the one who became closed and limited. On the other hand, when I accepted new opportunities, even with uncertainty about how Trent would respond or handle the experience, I discovered an improvement in both Trent's situation and my own life. In other words, I liked the feeling of empowerment, which allowed me to see that my perceptions and choices carried Trent on a particular path of growth.

What is often the main support for an individual with DD, including severe ASD?

Family is the foundation of support and security for many individuals with severe disabilities (Callahan & Garner, 1997). Diverse ways to support families must be explored, designed, and created. Individuals with DD who are in the transition phase rely on their families and continue to be involved with them on a daily basis (Mallory, 1995).

What contributions can families make to their child's growth in adult life?

The family is usually aware of the young adult's interests and are often key advocates regarding a vision of assisted community life (Turnbull et al., 1996). A study of how students perceived family involvement found that young adults relied on parents, brothers and sisters, aunts, uncles, and grandparents for assistance in employment and housing (Morningstar, Turnbull, & Turnbull, 1995).

What are community life outcomes for young adults when a family becomes involved?

The opportunities that a person with a severe disability receives during his or her adult life is often dependent upon the family's involvement (Callahan & Garner, 1997).

What is known about the connection between a child's disability and family stress?

Demands on the family to care for a child with ASD or other disabilities place increased stress on families (Gray & Holden, 1992; Konstantereas, Homatidis, & Plowright, 1992; Marquette, 2001; Sharpley, Bitsika, & Efremidis, 1997; Singer & Irvin, 1991). Families are often disconnected from the community because of issues related to their care-giving role (Covert, 1992).

Families experience much greater stress when the child reaches adulthood. Due to limited resources, many individuals and their families reluctantly accept a less appropriate or desired service because it is the only choice. Programs are often restrictive and sheltered. Therefore, the young adult's post-high school outcomes may not be true preferences (Kosciulek, 1999).

What are young adults' reactions to their transition when they live isolated day by day?

Some young adults have no access to services and no opportunities to have a productive day, participate in the community, or become involved in relationships. These adults may engage in increased repetitive, obsessive behaviors that tend to dominate the life of their family. The individual's disruptive behaviors are likely to increase because there is no other community outlet or service options available (Hayden, Spicer, Depaepe, & Chelberg, 1992).

Wing (2001) reported that the longer a behavior occurs in these cases, the less the person is interested in leaving the home. The solution for both the individual with ASD and the family is an appropriate residential service that offers community participation and activities (Wing, 2001). I would like to expand upon Wing's claim. For those with ASD or DD who are confined to the home because of an inability to control obsessions, the behavior becomes a self-perpetuating cycle. That is, the more they participate in the behavior, the less they are able to adapt in the home or elsewhere. I lived this experience with Trent and saw that when he fell into this downward spiral, he lacked structure for other meaningful things and a purpose each day. I began to see how he craved something more in his life, not just a regimented list of tasks to do but meaning and a desire to belong as well. These anchors are essential to function, but more than that, to grow personally.

What factors limit student transitions?

Schuster, Timmons, and Moloney (2003) conducted a study to determine employment factors that influence the transition planning process and the development of goals and dreams for young adults with disabilities and their families. The researchers conducted in-depth, unstructured interviews with parents and students to gain their perspectives. A total of 10 parents and 12 students participated, representing a wide range of disabilities.

Five factors were found to interfere with the transition planning process: (a) poor job matches, even though students were aware of their skills and interests; (b) an apparent lack of partnership between families and schools; (c) limited social supports to support employment and continuing education opportunities; (d) anxiety over present circumstances and uncertainty about the future; and (e) family financial limitations.

How have families become involved?

According to Callahan and Garner (1997), the results of the transition phase may lead to family involvement expressed in these forms:

- The family surrenders to the unquestioned expertise of the professional and the decision-making power of professionals.
- The family representing the individual accepts the fact that no help is available.
- The family assumes the role of professionals because other forms of support are not available.
- The family interacts with professionals to achieve outcomes that are supportive for the individual with a disability.

The last of these is optimal. Families can engage in this interactive strategy by initiating or participating in a Person-Centered Planning (PCP) committee (Mount, 2000).

What do we know about quality of life for individuals with a DD?

Experiencing the freedom to make choices and have control over our lives are major quality-of-life indicators for all of us, including individuals with disabilities (Stancliffe & Parmenter, 1999).

Nancy Dalrymple, a national expert on autism, a colleague and friend, once pointed out to me that quality of life is "being comfortable and accepted within the community and being treated as an individual."

Being part of the community means having the opportunity to interact and form relationships with other community members. To be part of the community is to be a family member, neighbor, schoolmate, friend, church member, shopper, coworker, and significant other (Kosciulek, 1999).

Community living means having the right to be known as an individual or a unique person. It does not, however, carry the burden of being labeled a ward of the state, a client of an agency, or the recipient of another's altruistic acts (Taylor, Bogdan, & Racino, 1991).

Independence should be measured according to the individual's quality of life with adequate supports. That quality is not measured by the tasks one performs without assistance (Marquette & Miller, 2004; Ward, 1996).

CHAPTER TWO
ROLE OF
THE PROFESSIONAL

Gifts and Strengths in Student Transition

*"Transition" is the creating and building of
a person's life by integrating the past
and present into the future.*

Educators and other human service professionals play a powerful role in helping students achieve successful transitions to post-high school life. The transition plan starts for the student at age 16 at the latest; it involves a team of professionals, the family/advocate and, most important, the young adult him/herself as a main participant. The professionals include anyone who is involved in treatment, makes recommendations, or educates youth with ASD or DD. This may include any or all of the following:

- teachers
- paraprofessionals

- speech therapists
- occupational therapists
- counselors or other forms of therapists
- coaches or leaders in particular activities of interests (e.g., after-school enrichment programs)
- vocational rehabilitation counselors
- university or college disability departments
- employment providers and job coaches
- agency representatives who provide supports for community living
- community coaches

Often educators and other professionals do not hear how they have made positive contributions to the transition and quality of life of their students. In my own research, parents commented over and over again that the teachers from the past were a major support of their child's growth, not just academic, but personal and emotional as well.

Here are some examples.

- A young man with Asperger Syndrome was ridiculed excessively by classmates for years. Yet, when a high school teacher saw his artistic gift, she encouraged him and offered guidance and support that developed his confidence. He started off making posters for the football team and then entered a contest and landed the top 50 out of 30,000 entries. He won first place, and his painting sold for $6,000.00. "For the first time in his life he achieved acceptance and commendation," his mother said.

- A young woman was taught facilitative communication at the age of 13 by a very committed speech teacher. Today she co-teaches a workshop with a speech teacher and attends college.

- A mother claims that her son's teachers were wonderful and that the parent-teacher relationship was extremely good.

- A social studies teacher had a huge impact on a young man's awareness of the world, socially. Because of that teacher, the dad says his son has acquired an empathetic view of certain social issues.

- A young man's school experiences throughout the years have been mostly positive. His mother expressed that he had wonderful teachers who were great resources.

No doubt, students' successes are dependent, to a large extent, upon educators and other professionals. Indeed, their successes do not happen by accident! Our role as educators has been and continues to be, broadly, to prepare youth for post-high school life through instruction and assessment. Policy, to include IDEA, has set the ultimate roadmap for a student's life after high school. Briefly, the process is driven by the students' goals, objectives, and other coordinated transition activities.

The key outcomes that determine students' transition success include employment (matching interests and contributions to the job), participation in college or training programs, and independent living. Unfortunately, independent living is often overshadowed by the other two outcomes — employment and training. Yet, the goal to live on one's own apart from family, including in an assisted living program, is critical. Thus, we, the professionals, must ask: "How well are students with ASD and DD making the transition to live with as much independence as possible?"

Community living is unanimously recognized among professionals and researchers as "best practice." Most persons with disabilities, however, continue to live with their family years into adult life (Blue-Banning & Turnbull, 2002). The dream of becoming more independent of family members is difficult and rarely occurs for those with moderate to severe disabilities. It is critical that school districts, along with human service agencies, establish approaches and policies to teach self-advocacy and provide information as well as training and support to students and their families about the transition phase, including finding employment, navigating the system, and acquiring governmental resources.

The provision of transition services is often confusing and intimidating to families. The schools are the ideal place to pass information about post-high school services and options to students and their families. School personnel can also help empower individuals and families as they become the support and advocate for the young adult during post-high school years. Increasing successful transitions in youth must be a high priority.

Increasing Successful Transitions

*"There is the risk you cannot afford to take, [and]
there is the risk you cannot afford not to take."*
— Peter Drucker

The above quote can be applied to student transition, and as such reveals a need to develop a perspective that reinforces innovative practices that increase successful transition for all students, including both those who are high functioning and those with more severe challenges. Current efforts are rooted in good intentions that help youth attain integrative employment, develop independent skills, and live independently. However, these practices generally target high-functioning students and young adults while excluding those who are more severely involved, who tend to end up in day programs and sheltered employment settings.

When policy and practice are not developed to provide support so people with disabilities can have quality of life, we run a risk of preventing people from entering and enjoying community life and living basic, ordinary lives. Examples of quality of life that all persons with disabilities deserve include something as "basic" as:

- shopping at the grocery store
- attending church
- going to a baseball game
- living in an apartment alone or with a roommate
- caring for one's own belongings and self-care
- enjoying a hobby
- owning a house
- employment in a job with a good match to interests and skills with supports
- managing money
- making choices on purchases
- setting goals
- planning a vacation
- taking an evening class or going to college part or full time

While support will be needed to participate in or access these settings, they are attainable goals for many. By contrast, sheltered programs limit the person's access to typical peers and community settings and also reinforce the notion that his or her disability need is too great to get out and enjoy community just as the rest of society does.

Students and their families must be provided knowledge about community living and strategies that make it possible. Many families reluctantly accept sheltered programs because they are not aware that integrative employment opportunities may be a realistic option for the young adult. If a family is not aware of options for inclusion, how can they guide the young adult and make a choice?

In the past decades, students with severe disabilities have been afforded the right to participate and be included with typical peers in general education. Their families have seen the positive effects of these experiences, and to step backward into only sheltered programs for the family member is not an option many would choose.

Professionals must offer students and their families a process for creating opportunities. How do we begin? A first step is to disseminate information to families about all the options available and provide training to increase understanding and knowledge. We can develop an organizational vision that draws on collaboration between school personnel, other professionals, and families, which may include school districts, adult service agencies and/or disability organizations. School districts and human service agencies can realistically and positively improve the transition of students and their families to post-high school life.

The next section will explore more possibilities and options that can take youth through the change into successful post-high school life.

Policy Development to Empower Students

School personnel and other professionals must coordinate and develop programs that emphasize and increase student self-awareness of specific skills, interests, and gifts, and/or build personal strengths. These are the how-to pieces essential for the Walking the Path model to work. The strategies can be developed and applied across statewide school systems, within school districts, special education programs, or school-based programs, or be individually implemented by one teacher who sees the value and connection to improve a student's situation in the transition phase.

These activities increase adolescents' self-worth and self-determination and can provide connective links to leisure, employment, and relationships. Equally important, by using their strengths constructively, students can work around their limitations. For example, a student who exhibits a strong interest in citizenship can be shown ways to apply that interest in volunteer work or paid employment. Quite often family members are main supports in negotiating and establishing resources to assist young adults in participating in the community (Turnbull et al., 1996). It is imperative that professionals develop projects within the school curriculum that facilitate interagency and family collaboration.

The suggestions offered below are designed to increase successful student transition and build continuing life support through the following activities: (a) Student Activity and Projects, (b) Interagency/Community Projects, and (c) Parental/Professional Collaborative Projects. All variables, in combination, can help students manage the transition years with higher levels of adaptive success

Student Activities and Projects

1. *Coordinate and develop programs* that emphasize a student's self-awareness regarding how skills, strengths, and gifts can be identified and used for leisure, employment, or careers. Offer students a variety of activities that build self-worth through exploration of gifts. These activities can challenge the person's growth and stretch his imagination about who and what he can become.

2. *Offer after-school enrichment programs in the arts.* Arrange for gifted students to teach students with disabilities through the exploration process of identifying and using strengths, gifts, and talents. Offer the gifted students community service credit and/or a grade for a class project on what they discovered and learned, thereby encouraging and promoting their personal growth.

3. *Guide students to set goals.* Make it easy for students to see the link between goals they set for themselves and positive outcomes. For example, "You've saved half of your allowance each week, and now you have $625.00 in the bank. It won't be long before you have enough to buy the computer you want." This strategy can be applied in every area of living; the applications are endless. Students need to see the value in setting a long-term goal. They need to see a process for reaching a goal by breaking it into several short-term objectives. Lead students through planning activities to determine sequential steps. Most important, help them see how their efforts are moving them closer to their goals.

4. *Prepare for careers.* Offer students experiences to observe, participate in, and evaluate careers they want to pursue. Allow students to enter the community and see the career in action.

5. *Promote self-advocacy.* Foster student self-advocacy by developing activities in curriculum and special projects that allow plenty of practice. Assist students in advocating or speaking on their own behalf. For example, learning how to ask for help in areas of academics and social situations is self-empowering. The student may recognize that she needs assistance in remembering the steps in her task/job and may learn to ask the boss for permission to use a note pad (an accommodation) to jot down the steps/altered work plan. Examine other areas of self-advocating such as in vulnerable student confrontations, including bullying, ridicule, and so on.

6. *Explore post-high school training.* Assist the student in obtaining information about planning and preparing for college entry or other postsecondary training.

7. *Teach the student how to make choices.* Students need to recognize how making conscious decisions impacts their lives. Provide them numerous opportunities to make choices during day-by-day activities across all areas of living. Ideas include forming academic goals, exploring careers, planning schedules, recognizing the benefits of diet and sleep habits, and so on.

8. *Provide supports and adaptations.* Identify assistive technology and "people supports" that have worked in increasing the student's adaptation to learning or functioning in diverse settings.

9. *Offer information.* Seek out transition information you can offer the students and families you serve.

10. *Address student behavioral issues.* Differentiate between the student's capabilities and his behavior. It is sometimes presumed that a student's level of functioning and/or behavioral issues will hinder adaptation to a community setting or success at a job. As I worked to create employment opportunities for students with severe disabilities, our team learned that a student's disruptive behaviors often diminished significantly when work related to the student's interests and enjoyment occurred.

Interagency/Community Projects

11. *Provide training.* Offer inservice to school personnel on student awareness and self-discovery of skills, strengths, and gifts.

12. *Develop community partnerships.* Coordinate with area businesses to establish collaborative career exploration and work opportunities for students. Develop interagency partnerships (student employment and mentorship programs) with local companies.

13. *Determine post-high school outcomes.* Conduct follow-up study after graduation on outcomes of student employment, college, training, and independent living. Ask how often youth are graduating to outcomes where they are moving upward and forward to live with greater independence, even with supports and assistance by others.

14. *Pass information on to students and their families.* Retrieve information from agencies about procedures for student entry in post-high adult vocational rehabilitation programs and services. Identify transition services to include supports offered by community agencies.

15. *Identify supports and adaptations.* Retrieve information about supports and accommodations for students with disabilities offered in postsecondary programs, colleges, and universities. Provide training about such supports.

16. *Offer transition fairs or other awareness events.* Invite agencies and colleges to deliver a short presentation and provide information about their services. Invite employment agencies and businesses leaders. Make announcements through the media and encourage the entire community to attend. The more proactive you are with all aspects of the community, the more success you will have in drawing in attendees.

Parent-Professional Collaborative Projects

17. *Recognize that the family is the student's main support for options in post-high school life.* Validate parental concerns and assist families in preparing for the young adult's transition by disseminating information about resources and services. Offer families strategies that support their role in guiding the young adult to create and choose community participation and involvement. While the service system and personnel fluctuate, the family is constant. These are turbulent times for both the individual and the family. Families need this new information as it enables them to recognize options and make choices through the transition process.

18. *Communicate.* Develop policy for creating ways to improve communication between school personnel and family.

19. *Show patience.* Practice showing patience toward families who may have strong concerns about the young adult's educational program. Some parents push loudly for the educational resources the student needs for two reasons: (a) the educational service or support is perceived as being of high value in the student's life after high school; and (b) deep down, parents fear the unknown of the post-high school years and what those years will bring. Know that these reactions are normal and respond accordingly.

20. *Listen.* Use good listening skills when communicating with families. It is easy for both professionals and parents to make assumptions about the other party's intent (i.e., what they really mean but aren't saying, subtle messages behind their looks or body language, etc.). Also, avoid creating communication barriers by appreciating diverse cultures, language differences, sex, upbringing, and physical and emotional makeup.

21. *Offer positive feedback.* Express to families the strengths and capabilities you notice in the child/student. Parents need to hear positive feedback from professionals. Be honest about the supports and resources the student may need in order to explore and use his gifts in diverse areas of living, including domestic, community settings, employment, or college.

22. *Provide training on "professional-family collaboration."* Offer school personnel professional training regarding strategies to increase family participation in the full transition planning process for the student.

23. *Offer parental training.* Offer ongoing parental training on various topics related to transition that impact a student's as well as her family's life. Include the preparation for the student's/family's emotional role change for post-high school living. Invite a counselor to present a process that can lead the young adult to greater independence, growth, and maturity. Help the student and her family discover and apply their own strengths. Also encourage and facilitate family-to-family support and networking. Offer these opportunities when families are receptive and secure, the earlier the better. Don't wait until families are overwhelmed and threatened with few options.

24. *Arrange events*. Host fun events such as a transition fair to bring students and families useful information about post-high school options. Be proactive in offering information about exploring options and establishing supports for post-high school life.

25. *Offer options*. Be open to actions you can initiate under your personal control as a teacher or other professional. Offer families information about options for life after high school that they may have not recognized. At times, family advocates are at a loss, because they see so few options for their young adult. Offer encouraging information to families from this book and/or other resources. Invite agency representatives to student transition meetings and introduce them to the student and family so the professional will get to know the client's desires and goals.

26. *Act in good faith with students and their families*. With the act of creating new community options come risks and obstacles that create "fear" in both the student and the family. Many families are not open to creating options, but if just a few access information and make attempts that turn out to be successful, the positive examples show others the way. Actions to get started include person-centered-planning to identify goals, strengths, and resources; hiring a community coach; finding job tasks that are enjoyable yet challenge the student's ability; and building natural supports in employment.

27. *Collaborate with families*. Work collaboratively with families and encourage their follow-up with self-determined activities for their child at home. Teach parents to recognize when they habitually protect their child from consequences — the message that the child receives is that parents do not believe she can learn from the lesson. In addition, when we (parents) ignore our children's problems, we are undermining their ability to pull through difficult times. Young adults are more capable of handling emotional setbacks when they know they have support and someone to lean on.

28. *Respect family diversity and strengths*. Honor the racial, cultural, and socioeconomic diversity among families. Recognize and point out family strengths and individualities. Offer meaningful projects during transition planning and program development that involves both families and professionals.

29. *Provide resources.* Help families to access emotional support through the transition years. By helping the family learn a process for navigating the transition process and make decisions that support growth in the young adult, you empower the young adult and the family to believe they can create options.

30. *Facilitate parent-professional collaboration.* Develop collaborative projects at all levels of the student's individual program through implementation and evaluation of services and programs, as well as policy formation.

31. *Conduct systemic evaluations.* Determine family needs that assist the transition of the student/young adult.

In summary, designing collaborative projects is the key to promoting a kind of collective effort that maximizes successful transition for youth with disabilities. The strategies discussed here can help youth recognize a gift or strength and develop a higher self-awareness and confidence, which, in turn, can open doors in terms of leisure, employment, or college attendance. Equally important, these recommendations draw in the family. This is critical because the family will need as much help as possible to advocate and guide their young adult after high school.

Youth and their parents have commented how significantly certain teachers or professionals have impacted their lives. Start out by trying a handful of the 31 strategies suggested here. Let it be a start, a commitment to alter student outcomes. Successful transition outcomes do not happen by accident! They are dependent upon educators and/or professionals, in addition to students and their families.

CHAPTER THREE
ROLE OF THE FAMILY

Increasing the Adolescent/Young Adult's Capability and Independence

The day you learned your child has autism [disability] is nothing compared to the day you observe him safely living out life with purpose, well-being, and among peers.

Can you see your son or daughter in a place where he or she is accepted and growing as an individual? A place where the young adult will not only occupy time but discover an interest, strength, or gift to be useful in some way? Your young adult, regardless of the severity or type of disability, has a purpose and is meant to contribute something useful to the community. That purpose can be found through his skills, gifts, strengths, or interests. This outcome is realistic, whether your son or daughter is in a day program, is about to leave high school, or has three or more years of school left. Start where you are, wherever that may be. The Walking the Path (WP) model presented here will guide you.

Many individuals with ASD and DD are living their lives with purpose, acceptance, and increased independence. If this is your family's desire, much is required from you, the parent/guardian, and others to bring it out. But it is possible. You may need to negotiate for additional supports and find new opportunities for your young adult. This requires stepping out of your comfort zone, which can be difficult. How do you get started? Again, the WP model will guide you.

Some parents are inclined to protect their adolescent/young adult from unpleasant experiences. That's only natural, but don't fear your young adult experiencing failure from trying. As long as the experiences teach and challenge, they are useful. I am not encouraging any experience that will put the individual in harm's way (e.g., crossing the street when training was not provided). The model will teach the family how to develop a perspective to establish supports to help the young adult step out and explore. Honor the individual's right to try new roles and actions that promote growth and independence.

This chapter offers a perspective and a process that I and many other families have found successful. It is important that you read this chapter before beginning the activities with your young adult in Chapter Four. I wish I could guarantee you a certain outcome for your young adult, but I cannot. I promise, however, that if you are willing to do the activities, you will discover insights that will help ground your beliefs and increase both your child's and your family's well-being.

Read and consider the questions presented in this chapter. Your family and your son or daughter are about to embark upon a new way of living with new roles. Based on my research and my personal experiences with my son Trent, the information in this chapter can help prepare you for your new role as a parent of an adult with ASD. No one has shown parents how to do this. There is not a right or wrong way to work through this chapter. Read and reflect on one activity a day or read through all of them, later carefully taking time to reflect. Take your time.

Rethinking Our Perceptions of Persons with Disabilities and Family

Believe that life is worth living, and your belief will help create that fact.
— William James (as cited in Dyer, 2001, p. 143)

When we view ourselves or see individuals with disabilities and their families by the descriptions in the first column, we operate from a point of fear. None of these negatives needs be true. Consider the alternative views in the second column for your child/young adult and your family.

Individuals with Disabilities and Their Families Are:	Individuals with Disabilities and Their Families Can Be:
dependent	lifted by accepting support
crazy	passionate and sane
poor	live flourished lives
living isolated	accepted
doomed	saved
alone with each other	among friends and associates
hopeless	hopeful
destined to failure	successful by using the discovery process
a drain to society and must be taken care of	productive, offering contributions to society
require experts to make decisions for their lives	make good choices

Society often sends implicit, negative messages that families cannot afford to absorb. Being aware of the negative and the positive is the purpose here, so you are prepared to fight stereotypes and empower yourself and your son or daughter.

Myths About Independence

It is important that we recognize what is a "truth" and what is a "myth" about releasing our bonds with our young adult to live with assistance apart from us. Below are some of the myths I once believed and that held me back and, therefore, denied my son certain opportunities. I learned that other families were releasing these myths as they guided their young adult to an independent life and, finally, had the courage to do the same myself.

- "My son isn't ready for independent assisted living; who will understand his needs without me around?"

- "My daughter has health issues; I am the only one who can take care of her."

- "We are a family and won't let a program or agency take our place with our child."

- "We'll think about it later in life, when I or my husband gets sick. What's the rush?"

- "My son is just too disabled. He has autism and cannot communicate his own needs."

- "Having a day program is just fine right now; my son has enough. The hours he goes to it will look like school. That's what we're used to."

- "The sheltered workshop down the street is convenient and my daughter has friends there."

- "It's too expensive and too risky."

- "It would mean changing our lives completely if my son lived apart from us. What would I do if he doesn't need me any more?"

Families who have led their young adult to independence have learned to recognize that low expectations actually became their reality. They also learned that when helping their young adult to reach for higher levels of involvement, the result was a more inclusive lifestyle.

Truth About Community or Independent Living

Below are comments other parents have made about their young adult living independently.

- "It was great; I got independent living, too."

- "I never knew the community could be so kind to my daughter. She loves her new living arrangement with two other women roommates who have become her friends."

- "Our sons have learned to keep their house clean, work, pay bills, and meet new people with whom they sometimes socialize after work."

- "So much growth has occurred. I never dreamed that my son could have problem solved, made decisions, and handled responsibilities."

- "Johnny loves having his own apartment and living his life freely. He drives, has a job, and makes his own purchases."

Examining Beliefs and Principles About Independence

It is important to set aside what others or society have told us or implied about where people with disabilities can live. The foundation that determines our vision and drives our decisions and actions is built upon our beliefs and principles. Beliefs refer to the *why* we live our lives. Principles refer to the *how* we live our lives. In other words, they are rules we follow as we take action.

Beliefs

Through this activity, it is important to recognize beliefs that you acted upon and that benefited you and your family. You may also find that you have certain beliefs that you have tucked away because society sent messages that they were unachievable. Beliefs *can be changed*. Often original beliefs are not really beliefs you chose yourself, but are based upon myths, societal prejudice, fear, or limited opportunities. Below are some beliefs I eventually learned to accept about inclusion and acceptance.

I believe:

- persons with disabilities do *not* have to live isolated and sheltered. It is essential that they have opportunities to associate and communicate with persons in a variety of community environments.

- each person with a disability has a purpose and is here to contribute something useful to our world. That purpose may take the form of a skill, a gift, the role of a participant or a spectator, an attitude that lifts others, a comforter, and yes, as simple as his or her presence.

- everyone needs to be loved ... and needs to know they are loved.

- people with disabilities can continually reach higher levels of personal involvement although it may require governmental and societal supports.

- every problem has a solution.

- in God.

- everyone needs family.

- that to love someone else, you must first know and love yourself. (This one is especially for moms.)

- in the importance of family and how family contributes to the life of the person with a disability.

- that it is never too late to learn something new or try something new.

- people have a basic desire to be accepted and loved.

- in not blaming others, recognizing my own mistakes, and then letting it all go.

- that privileges and responsibility go hand in hand.

- the only way to overcome the fear of loosening the strong bond to my child is through knowledge.

- when we stop growing, our human spirit dies.

Principles

As you approach your child's adult years, think of your principles as a shield or an armor that protects you and your family from events or people who act as blocks or obstacles. Let's look at the story at the end of this book, **Our Family's Journey**. As a parent guiding your son or daughter to his or her independent life, you and the young adult cross the bridge in fear but with belief that something is better on the other side. Both of you take the first step off the bridge, and there you are on rocky ground. You walk carefully; your shield and boots are principles that protect you. In other words, the farther you travel, the stronger your principles about your adolescent's/young adult's independence will become.

My principles, developed over the years:

- I will keep learning the value of reaching new levels of involvement with my son's independence.

- I will reach out to others and search for supports that include my son in the community. I am open to exploring numerous supports, even those that I can create without governmental programs.

- I will help my son find a reason and a purpose to live, no matter how simple.

- I will choose a new role of involvement in my son's life — one that will assist him where and when he needs an advocate. I will resist directing his life according to my own preferences.

- I will seek to understand the benefits of "change" in my family's life and my son's adult life.

- On our journey to independence, I will keep an open mind and let go of anticipating a negative outcome.

- I will seek ways to enjoy my life separately from my son.

- I will seek ways he can enjoy his life separately from me.

- I will allow myself to make mistakes on this journey and learn from them.

- I will allow my son to have setbacks and learn from them.

- I will allow my son to grieve the loss of familiar persons and routines in his daily life and grow from it.

- I will accept that no one person can make my son's transition into adult life easy and successful. I will seek help from others.

- I will accept that some relationships cannot be repaired or replaced. I will recognize my losses and let go of previous hurts.

- I will be there for my son; however, my level of involvement may become less direct in order to release him to grow and change for his betterment.

- I will not blame others.

- I will accept responsibility.

- I will not isolate myself from others.

- I will find reasons to laugh.

What Are Your Beliefs?

Are you willing to take a closer look at your own beliefs? Consider some beliefs you may want to explore. This can be a bit intimidating, but having the courage to examine your beliefs is an important first step. In the space provided on the next page, list your current beliefs. Then list beliefs you may want to consider about your son/daughter's adult life.

My lists of beliefs and principles on the preceding pages may help you become aware of actions and routines that serve as beliefs and principles without your thinking explicitly about them. Many of these beliefs and principles may exist without your conscious awareness.

Current Beliefs

_____

_____

_____

_____

_____

_____

_____

_____

_____

_____

_____

_____

_____

_____

Current Beliefs

Revised Beliefs

_____

_____

_____

_____

_____

_____

_____

_____

_____

_____

_____

_____

_____

_____

_____

_____

What Are Your Principles?

List principles you have about your son/daughter's independent adult life. Then list principles you may want to consider incorporating/revising.

Current Principles

_____

_____

_____

_____

_____

_____

_____

_____

_____

_____

_____

_____

Revised Principles

_____

_____

_____

_____

_____

_____

_____

_____

_____

_____

_____

_____

_____

_____

Taking Ownership

If you bravely recognize your beliefs and principles, one day you will find that your beliefs, principles, and actions become increasingly aligned. You will see your young adult and your family living your highest dreams. Don't allow fear and over-protectiveness to drive your decisions in life. Be honest with yourself.

As I progressed with Trent along our journey, I eventually realized that I often told myself lies that prevented me from facing our life's direction. I remember thinking "Trent is really better off living with me. He needs *me* to know what he desires." Yes, it is true your young adult needs you, but in a much different way than when he was younger.

Identifying Mental Blocks

Life for the young adult can be rough and confusing at times, but it has the potential to become better than the school days. Although limited governmental resources present an obstacle to accessing supports and assistance to active community living, we as parents may be limiting the young adult's opportunities as well by hanging on to worn-out beliefs that do not serve us any longer. An example of a worn-out belief includes relating to the young adult just as you did when she was a child.

If your adolescent is just entering adulthood, it may be difficult to see a hopeful future; yet, it is important to *imagine* the young adult's new adult life with independence and a purpose. You may be thinking that having an imagination is silly and only for children. Read these quotes from Albert Einstein on imagination and you may change your mind.

"Imagination is more important than knowledge."
Albert Einstein

"The intellect has little to do on the road to discovery. There comes
a leap in consciousness, call it intuition or what you will,
and the solution comes to you and you don't know how or why."
Albert Einstein (as cited in Gillman, 1996, p. 53)

I gradually learned that the ideas that led Trent through the transition into his new independent-assisted life began with my imagination. The questions on the next page are essential to ask. I offer them as a guide to consider as you face your child's new adult life.

Imagine an Ideal Life

Imagine the most ideal life for your young adult. Imagine the most ideal life for yourself, too.

If you could wave a magic wand and an ideal life appeared for your young adult, what would it be? Can you visualize it?

Take time to reflect and just imagine a good life for the individual living his/her life as an adult. What would that resemble?

_____

_____

_____

_____

_____

_____

_____

_____

_____

_____

Evaluate Possibilities

Arrange whatever pieces come your way.
— Virginia Woolf

As your son's or daughter's guide, you will become like the mother or father bird who gently nudges the baby bird out of the nest when the time is right. Your eyes and ears are your antennas that lead you to clues for how to guide the young adult. Be open to possibilities and opportunities from which the young adult may benefit, even ideas you never considered before.

I recall finding activities and people in the most unlikely ways coming into Trent's life, such as a helpful high school job coach or an unexpected service referral made through a friend. As you begin to network, negotiate, and carve supports, new ideas to help your son or daughter explore will begin to emerge. My intention is to not oversimplify this process, but to point out that things can happen when one least expects. It is important to have a willing and ready attitude. The following questions will help you assess how ready and willing you are to explore new possibilities.

1. If the opportunity arrived at your doorstep for your daughter to have a job in a business or a setting she would love, but your concerns about her coping skills are high, would you recognize this as an option to explore? Could you consider ways to find the support she needed? Would you be too closed or fearful to see it?

2. Let's say your young adult has a goal to live in his own apartment, get a job, or obtain training or education. Could you find ways to help him reach him reach his goal?

3. Could you bravely guide the young adult to a new opportunity, even if that meant letting her risk making a mistake, failing, or experiencing grief? For example, joining a gym despite her significant sensory issues.

4. Could you see a new beginning in all this that could positively impact the family as well? For example, allowing more freedom and enjoyment for everyone.

5. If you had a chance to improve you own life, what would it be? We as parents must take care of ourselves, especially if we are caregivers. How do you give back to yourself?

I remember being available for the care of my son the majority of my time so that I rarely met with friends or family members. This is common among families, especially those who care for a young adult with a severe disability. If this applies to you, what options could you consider to explore that would connect you to friends, family members, or your spouse?

6. Can you accept developing a new relationship with your child who is now an adult? Consider how that would be different.

7. Can you be grateful for the journey that is behind you? Ahead of you?

8. Can you try to let go of all the hurts you observed in your young adult's past? They may be hindering your present life.

9. Can you trust that the journey ahead will be worth all the obstacles (the bumpy road) that may occur, resulting in disappointment?

10. Can you focus on the gifts you discovered in your son or daughter and recognize how they may lead to peace for the young adult or your family?

11. The outcome of trying to guide son or daughter to new opportunities versus settling for isolation should be viewed as "doing your best." Can you accept that no matter what the outcome is, peace comes from knowing that you have done everything possible? Can you recognize that these efforts become gifts that bring joy and happiness for you and other family members?

Managing Parental Fear

I recall devoting much attention during Trent's transition years, from age 19 to 23, to networking to create supports for him to participate in an activity/job. Sometimes these contacts brought unexpected opportunities, but there were times when I was blind to these possibilities.

Fear stifles the imagination and paralyzes actions. I understand now that I almost missed out on taking advantage of resources because I could not envision arrangements that went beyond the status quo. Even when I recognized the potential of an opened door, I recall hesitating to accept it.

For example, I remember when Troy, Trent's job coach, referred Jason as a community coach for Trent. At the time, I hid his name and phone number in a drawer. Six months later, Troy called again and suggested that Jason would be really good for Trent and that he could see them living together; according to Troy, they had compatible personalities. This time I did follow through, but my only consideration was that Jason would be a community coach. In reality, it worked out so well that a few months later, I asked Jason if he would be willing to be a live-in assistant. Trent and Troy have now been roommates and friends for seven years.

Why do we as parents reject new and unfamiliar options? Sometimes we simply cannot imagine anything that is drastically different from what we are comfortable with. And even if we see possibilities, we sometimes hold on due to fear of the unknown. I finally came around with the help of others. The lesson that I learned is that my answered prayers involved living with uncertainty and accepting personal responsibility.

So the question comes up, "When we get what we have been asking for, are we going to see it? grab it?" Sometimes reality looks very different from what we imagined.

Just as I discovered my own fears about Trent's safety, families have told me of similar concerns about their children. We seldom say to our child, "Try it and see what happens." Many parents have expressed that they believe their children are too limited to achieve independence because they can't express their needs well. One mother said, "I don't see how independent living could be for my son." I believed this, too, until I chose to see Trent's independence with supports of people around as good for him, and for myself. One mother commented shortly after her daughter began living independently with a roommate, "I got independent living, too."

Becoming agitated by dwelling on possible negative results of the young adult attending college, getting a competitive job, or spending a night or weekend away from home has no benefit. I recall a colleague telling me that her sister had a 7-year-old son with autism. She needed relief and wanted someone to stay with her son while she did her laundry. I referred her to Trent's respite provider and the local comprehensive care center for assistance. I later heard that the mother never followed through with the call, even though the respite person I recommended lived in her neighborhood.

Is it possible that our children may be observing our cautionary actions and accepting our fears as their own? While not true in every case, it is worth examining.

Often when young adults find a way to express their dreams and interests, such as a career or preferred place to live, we parents tell them in subtle ways that they can't fulfill a particular desire or wish. When confronted with these reactions, our young adults may lack the ego strength to respond, "Wait a minute! I, too, can have a job and learn to ride the bus to get there."

When we were children ourselves and somebody asked us, "How do you know you can be a _____?" we may have stumbled over our words trying to explain. If we are honest with ourselves, most of us didn't know for sure we could reach any of our goals, but we didn't let that stop us. As parents we must examine our responses cautiously when the young adult exhibits an interest or voices a dream.

What Happens When We Focus on Our Fears?

Fear sometimes warns us of danger. Fear has a function and tells us to react for our own safety, such as getting out of the way if a car is coming toward us. But sometimes fear is beneath the surface. It feels cold, controlling, and hurtful. Sometimes what we don't know is what scares us. When we cannot see the good and the possibilities that action can offer, we become fearful. If we stay with this mindset, it becomes a closed and stagnating place.

I recall talking with a mother who would not allow her son to experience any community settings even with a willing support person because "something bad might happen." If the individual is to achieve adult status and live happily and with purpose, the goal itself must become the focus, not the fear of outcomes.

Take a closer look at fear. Are your fears protecting you, limiting you, guiding you? Some of our fears as parents are real, but some are not. Sometimes we have to push ourselves a little. For example, I feared letting Trent ride Tarc 3, a bus system in our community that offers door-to-door service for people with disabilities. However, I agreed to let Trent try it by arranging for specific notes to be attached to the bus driver's schedule about Trent and his communication limitations. I also arranged for a supervisor to meet Trent when he arrived at his job.

The bus ride proved successful. Now did I take a risk? Did Trent take a risk? Yes, most definitely. I try to calculate the risks before I make a decision. If the chance of harm or injury is high, I never take the risk. However, if an awkward moment, or even a slight uncomfortable situation or disappointment may be the result, that is a risk worth trying because it offers experience in living in this world and stretches my son to higher capabilities.

Evaluate Your Fears

*"You gain strength, courage, and confidence by every experience
in which you really stop to look fear in the face.
You must do the thing which you think you cannot do."*
— Eleanor Roosevelt

No one can tell you what is right; you are the judge. Take a step, however small, and act each day to face one of the fears you may have. As you release certain fears, you may notice that your son or daughter may progress and participate with increased capability. You may also see personal empowerment you didn't know was possible.

List your fears and consider these questions: Are they protecting the young adult from true harm? Are they holding your young adult back from experiencing personal growth? Is the outcome an experience that could be potentially harmful or just an awkward moment?

_____

_____

_____

_____

_____

_____

_____

_____

I suggested to a mother whose son was graduating from high school that she envision her son's first few years out of high school. I asked her, "What does your son want?" She said, "I'm not sure, but I just want him to be happy." Then I asked, "What does happy look like?" "I don't know; I'm too afraid to look," she answered. She was unwilling to let her son keep a paid job developed in school to help him graduate from high school because it interfered with Saturday morning family activities. The Saturday activities had been a tradition in the family for a long time, and fear of the unknown prevented change.

Why We Refuse New Opportunities

I have spoken with families who expressed wholeheartedly their worries for their young adult's participation in the community. These were families of students I worked with and families I met at disability conferences. Below are real-life situations. Names have been changed.

- Grace [daughter] is offered additional hours on her part-time job and has recently learned to ride the city bus, but her mom chooses to keep her at fewer hours so she can pick up her daughter after work, before mom has to be at work herself. She feared that harm would come to Grace if she allowed her daughter to ride the bus alone in order to work the added hours.

- Jack [son] is offered a Medicaid waiver to live independently with a highly respected provider agency who has been holding a spot for him. Mom says it is still not time, and puts it off.

- A respectable youth minister offers to be a community coach for Dale, a young man with autism who has occasional but significant obsessive behaviors. Dale's parents considered it, but put it off because of fear that something will happen when Dale is away from his family.

The above examples reflect parental fear of change. The change may seem too much to handle because the parent is not ready to accept the child's new options. I learned that I had to let myself be open to change first in order to encourage and allow Trent to grow. Just because a way of life or a structure was right for us yesterday (during the school years) does not mean it meets our needs today. People grow. People change.

Ask yourself if you are holding on to something that does not work any more for your son, your daughter, or yourself. If so, you may be fearful about your child experiencing new levels of growth or losing something from the past. Change often brings fear. Change can also bring sadness because of a loss of something familiar in the past.

What to Do When Change Hits

Individuals with disabilities experience some form of loss at the end of high school because of the abrupt change in schedules and routines. Families often experience a similar loss of their personal time because of the young adult's increased dependency, now that she is not in school most of the day. This is especially the case if the young adult has a severe disability. For example, work routines may be altered in families in order that someone is around to care for or spend time searching and negotiating resources and supports for the young adult.

How can the young adult recover from loss of the familiar routines of school, associations and friendships, and daily structures? How can we as parents help ourselves? Most important, how can we gain from this change initially perceived as loss? Is it possible that our loss can open new doors and new possibilities?

Some of Trent's losses included his parents' divorce, a move to another neighborhood, change of familiar routines that led to extra long days with little to do, three different jobs that didn't work, and less contact with his brothers. Trent responded to these disruptions by spiraling downward into obsessive compulsive behaviors and depression. The circumstances were so overwhelming that for a time I was also paralyzed. These reactions are common during post-high school life among families who have a young adult with developmental disabilities.

I am reminded that every end is a beginning. At the time it was difficult for me to see how these losses could serve Trent, or me. I couldn't see, because I focused on what we left behind. I grieved over our past lives. I discovered that my grieving was necessary, and the only way out of my trap was to look at what was just ahead.

If you are facing or soon will face your child's transition from high school, you will need a perspective that is supportive of your functioning and growth.

The Victim: Don't Ask, "Why Me?," Ask "What's Next?"

"Readjustment is a kind of private revolution."
— *Eleanor Roosevelt*

Wondering why we have to endure these challenges and sometimes asking "why me?" places us in the victim role. The good news is that something can be learned from the experiences and can lead us out of our present circumstances into a new and hopeful future. The right question to ask is "what's next?"

I recall not wanting Trent to experience failure or run into difficulties that would take both of us down. I wanted him to have the perfect life, with no pain. But life is not perfect. Setbacks and anguish are normal, and we grow as we face and overcome our challenges. That is just as true for those who are typical as for those who have a disability. In the early years I asked, "Why me?" "Why does Trent have to have autism?" Then I learned to ask a *different* question: "What's next?"

I learned to stop dwelling on my current troubles and focused instead on how those events could lead to a different circumstance. "OK, this is where Trent and I are today. How do I help Trent move from the life he has to a life with meaning, purpose, and growth? "What's next?"

By changing my question, I discovered daily examples of how Trent and I were progressing a bit. I learned that the key to our resiliency through these transition years was starting with this self-empowering question, "What's next?" Only by moving forward, even in small steps, with an open mind, did I discover fresh opportunities.

A Gain Disguised as a Loss

"In a dark time, the eye begins to see."
— *Theodore Rethke*

Recognizing that there can be something to "gain" even during a difficult time is an important tool that anyone can use in order to get unstuck and climb out of a "trench."

Brainstorm answers to the following questions. Recognize that the loss you experience today will not last. We have to replace our losses with new beginnings in life. Think of constructive actions that can be initiated, moving you and/or your young adult to an improved life.

Replacing Loss with New Beginnings

- How can a loss serve me?

- Where is the loss directing me?

_____

_____

_____

_____

_____

_____

_____

_____

_____

_____

_____

_____

The trick is to change pain into energy. For a time, I peered out the window on our future with neither imagination nor hope. Yet, as I began to read about how others overcame difficult challenges, I found that an underlying theme was the importance of believing that there is a silver lining. We must be willing to look at our situation and options differently. The solution may be that choice we once believed we would never find the courage to do. For example, I didn't think I could move out of our house where Trent and I lived and let his roommate move in, but I finally did.

The Young Adult's Anger

Quite often young adults experience anger due to confusion during the transition years. During puberty, huge biological changes take places in their bodies that can be frightening. Also, teachers and parents make more demands. All of this combines to create stress and confusion. No wonder, then, that youth with diverse disabilities are prone to experience more fears and anxiety during the transition stage, often resulting in anger and various kinds of manipulative behaviors.

Trent responded to his displaced life during the transition phase by ripping his shirts out of anger. He sometimes ripped three or four shirts in a 24-hour period during his blackest days. In the early years of post-high school transition, many individuals with disabilities, especially those with ASD, begin to exhibit behaviors of severe bouts of anger, obsessions, and depression.

Realistically, adolescents need more care and different types of support. During school and the post-high school years, medication is sometimes prescribed to control behavior or moods. Often this treatment is used rather than creating meaningful options that build self-development (Greenspan & Wieder, 2006), including activities such as those encouraged in this book that build and enhance personal growth.

Try This Perspective on Your Young Adult's Anger

Greenspan and Wieder (2006) offer solutions for dealing with the young adult's anger.

- Stay calm and regulate yourself. Encourage the teenager to be a collaborative problem solver.

- Meet his dependency needs with a chicken-soup approach. For example, arrange long car rides, validate his worries and concerns, listen to him talk about his feelings, and validate his worries and concerns. Offer a hopeful outlook with real plans and actions as well as constructive strategies to handle anger.

- Listen to his music, play the games he likes.

- Let him pretend to be more independent than he really is.

I learned that my son's anger was something I had to listen to. I chose to see his anger as a voice, a cry, a plea for him to be taken out of this place. Essentially, his anger reflected his fear and confusion about his old life dying and the pain of the unknown. Despair is an enemy in our lives. Anger, on the hand, is a friend. It was as if Trent was acting in his own best interest, the only way he knew, through anger. My job was to recognize it, interpret it, and help redirect Trent.

What Does Security Mean to Your Young Adult and Your Family?

Ask yourself what security means for your adult and your family. For me, the familiar security of having a roomy house full of my sons' loud funny voices and sports equipment lying around was no more. That definition didn't have meaning for me any longer after their school years ended. I have three sons; two attended college, one of them stayed in town and the other lived away. The third, Trent, was living with me. Trent's life became increasingly empty, as a great deal of his previous life was gone.

Moving to a modest house next door to my brother became my new security. After my husband and I separated, I learned that "security" had to be defined in a different way than before. I recognized actions that I could initiate by taking personal control in establishing a new security.

Which items on the following list do you view as security? What actions, however small, could you take toward reaching the security you want in your life, for your young adult? Some of these or others could be your goals. The purpose here is to know what goal you can set to determine your security and take a step forward to attain it.

- Predictability
- Trust fund established for your adult
- Being loved (young adult and your family)

- Good health

- Autonomy

- Being recognized or belonging to a group

- Freedom to choose

- Inner peace

- Physical strength

- Emotional strength — motivation to move through challenges, step by step

- Physical safety

- People to count on

- Trust

- Honesty

- Praise/acceptance

- Friends/family

- Owning a home

- An accepting environment

It is unlikely you will choose all of these to create security for your young adult or your family. The activity is intended to help you recognize and take steps toward establishing your security.

What Do You Value?

Everyone has values. Do you know what your values are? Do the decisions you make about guiding your young adult and your family's life reflect your values? Take time to see how clear your values are. Before developing a vision for your child and your family, you need to determine your values. Values are very personal.

As part of the transition process for my son, I began to look to my values with each and every decision I made as it applied to Trent and his independent life. For example, when Jason agreed to work as Trent's live-in roommate, I was the one who left the house and moved into an apartment. Friends and family questioned why I did not stay in the house and opt for Trent and Jason to move into an apartment. I responded that Trent was facing this major change in life of not living with me any longer and that staying in a house that he was famil-iar with offered him one less hurdle in the middle of the big new change. Furthermore, he would have his Uncle Craig next door, who would provide some support — both minor and im-mediate in case of an emergency. I valued the supports that made Trent's new independent life comfortable or doable for him.

> *"We always attract into our lives whatever we think about most,*
> *believe in most strongly, expect on the deepest level,*
> *and imagine most vividly."*
> *— Shakti Gawain*

I learned about my values when I began in-depth personal reflection. If you try this activity and take action each day, you will discover new insights that will help guide you and your young adult to options and solutions. Quality of life for the young adult is reached by pro-moting a vision based on values.

You can do this by writing your thoughts in a journal. Don't write about what you did or what happened. Instead, focus on your perceptions about events. Again, there are no "right" or "wrong" answers. These are all open-ended questions. Each person's life looks different. The questions are designed to help you recognize areas that are going well and/or notice chang-es you want to make. Watch out for areas where you may unconsciously have made decisions that do not reflect your values.

Why all this reflection? The family is the main foundation of support for the young adult, and if he moves forward into a higher quality of life, he will need the guidance of the family. How we as parents look at the adolescent's capability and right to a quality of life is signifi-cant to the young adult accessing these options. And that's where values come in.

Write daily about how you reacted to events, circumstances and people, professionals you work with, specifically those who assist or teach your son or daughter.

- What are thoughts about your present circumstances?

- What do you do each day? (What routines related to the event?)

- How do you feel each day?

- What captures your thoughts and imagination?

- Whom do you admire? Why?

- Whom do you choose to spend time with?

- What do you read about each day?

- What values do you want your children to have?

- What leaves you sad?

- What makes you angry?

- What do you stand for as a person? I learned that as Trent's mom, I stood for values that reflected a goal of my son having a daily purpose (a job), meaning (routine of chores and living with responsibility at home and in the community), and enjoyment (painting in his studio, meeting other artists, belonging to a church).

- What beliefs guide you?

- What values motivate you?

- What gives you energy?

Suppose you find, through careful reflection, that you are uncomfortable with current circumstances for the young adult as well as yourself. How do you begin taking steps forward, encouraging your young adult as well? What if you are just surviving day-to-day? I know well how that feels, but I think very few people, even other family members, know how trapped the parent can feel. But there is hope.

Lift Yourself out of a Mere Survival Mode

What do you do? All you see are closed doors? You may find yourself or your young adult in a slump, preferring to watch TV or expressing anger because he/she is trapped at home with no help and no prospects of a job or education.

Sometimes there is not enough help or hours in a day to meet the needs of the young adult in transition or even for families to care for their own needs. Parents may be trying to get the young adult in a program or on a waiting list for a service, but what do you do with the young adult while waiting for a service?

This is not the time to panic or despair. Panic and desperation will lead to bad judgment and flawed choices. This is a time to reach out for help from a loved one or a friend, and to trust God or a higher being perhaps. I found these steps helpful when Trent and I were living through those black days.

1. Take life one day and one need at a time. That means our needs as parents, too. Carve out part of your day just for you even if it is only an hour or a few minutes at a time. This is critical. I remember taking time to give back to myself; just going to the bookstore or a coffee shop alone meant a lot.

2. Do your part to use survival skills positively. Stay with schedules and involve your young adult in household routines. Find a support group (see Appendix G, Resources).

3. Strive for an attitude of responsibility for both your young adult and yourself. What can the young adult do daily to act upon responsibility, such as house chores, personal care, grooming? Involve your son or daughter in the home or in the community, one small step at a time.

4. Know that possibilities to change your life from day to day are not limited by your past or present circumstances. Keep your vision on your future. That is where change occurs.

5. Examine any attitude blocks that might prevent a solution from flowing into our young adult's life or your own life. I had such blocks. Do your fears limit your young adult's experiences?

   Some or none of the following may apply to you. Do you prevent your young adult from going out and participating in an activity with a friend or neighbor? Do you rely only on restrictive programs that separate individuals with disabilities, confining them inside walls? Are there any inclusive services you can explore? Do you prevent your young adult from trying integrated employment because of your fear for safety, etc.? Can you take small steps to loosen those strong bonds to your child?

Do not let a fearful attitude justify socially isolating your adult and family. Do your part today, however small. Choosing to hire a woman to stay with Trent for a few hours a day was my first step forward. Find the courage to take action, to let go of fear, and to trust the process so everyone can begin to experience growth.

Stay True to Your Values and Your Vision

How do we stay true to our values and vision while we seek a *remarkably able* life for our young adult? When I examined this concept, I saw how I allowed others' negative responses to impress, limit, or sadden me. I saw how the students I taught and their families also struggled in this area. Try the activity below to see how words create images that fill our minds.

Read the following list of words. Write descriptions of each word that immediately enters your mind.

- glowing _____

- secure _____

- content _____

- confident _____

- imaginative _____

- creative _____

- happy _____

Now read the list of words below. Write descriptions of the word that immediately enters into your mind.

- ashamed _____

- isolated _____

- frustrated _____

- confused _____

- listless _____

- hunger for meaning _____

We often give in unconsciously to the latter list and believe that our lives resemble these defined roles that we are destined to live. Why? I think it is because these words represent what we mainly see in the current lives of people with disabilities and their families. The secret to abandoning the roles in the last list is to find ways of living that are the opposite. If we take charge and do our part in choosing new actions, then we refuse to play out negative roles in our lives and replace them with new actions.

Choosing Optimism

I strongly encourage you to be optimistic about your work as parents/advocates. However, I recognize that it is difficult to be continually upbeat when our efforts to help young adults find employment, housing, and friends are compounded by countless obstacles. Finding the energy and willingness to move forward takes courage. How do we avoid giving up? How do we stay optimistic and focused on our goals in the midst of limited resources?

According to Gerber (2002), optimism means taking risks, confronting our fears, and pushing through with our attempts, regardless of the possibility of failure. "Optimism requires our mental discipline and is a worldview" (Gerber, 2002, p. 243). But how can I be positively hopeful at all times?

The message in this workbook is not about living in a fantasy world. I found Eleanor Roosevelt's answer helpful. She was asked why she wasn't more doubtful in a world full of trouble and despair (as cited in Gerber, 2002, p. 243).

> It is true that I am fundamentally an optimist, that I am congenitally hopeful. I do not believe that good always conquers evil, because I have lived a long time in the world and seen that it is not true. I do not seek the pot of gold at the foot of the rainbow or think that everything will have a happy ending because I would like it to. It is not wishful thinking that makes me a hopeful woman. Over and over, I have seen, under the most improbable circumstances, that man can remake himself, that he can even remake this world if he cares enough to try.

I have seen with my own eyes individuals with disabilities remake their world and sense of reality. Many have overcome seemingly impossible obstacles to achieve surprising successes. Quite often we recognize that it is difficult to find the energy to keep going and keep trying. But if we give up on ourselves or on the dreams that we have for our young adults, even partial success is not achievable.

Helen Keller said, "Although the world is full of suffering, it is also full of the overcoming of it." In the midst of all the negative scenes in our world, I try to focus on what these two remarkable women have thought and experienced.

Taking the journey is about initiating one step at a time. All we need is to have enough information to take the next step. All of my writings, including this workbook, are a paper trail of the steps Trent and I took. They include ideas, questions, dreams, images, experiments, and exploration in the days of smooth sailing as well as those that were dark and uncertain. I relate this journey in hopes that what is true for Trent and other young adults can be true for you, too.

Events, Choices, and Outcomes — Walking Our Path

The next pages show a chart of events that Trent and I faced during our transition to independent living. I provide this chart to illustrate the importance of aligning our beliefs and values when we are seeking solutions to goals. These events took place the last two years of Trent's high school career to a year after he had started living independently, within about a four-year time frame. You will see that we didn't continue on the path without stopping to rest. But I always found motivation to get back up and continue. Trent and I took a lot of risks and experienced failure and setbacks before success was noted.

When moving forward, there will be bumps and obstacles on the path, but know that staying on the course is all part of self-empowerment. Events, choices, and reactions listed are represented by T (referring to Trent) and J (for Jackie). You will see that events had an impact on both of us. Thus, the transition phase is not a linear process only impacting the student. It involves the entire family (Ferguson, Ferguson, & Jones, 1988).

EVENTS, CHOICES, AND OUTCOMES (an example)

Events	Choosing Beliefs and Principles	Outcome
T. Participated in his high school chorus, sang and performed for audience.	T. Found purpose and made a contribution.	T. exhibited enjoyment as he rocked to the beat of the music and sang, accepted in a group.
T. High school days	T. School setting offered routine schedule that was meaningful and purposeful.	T. Associated and participated with peers in integrative classes, (i.e., art, chorus).
T. Family activities	T. Wanted to be accepted and involved in day-by-day family and/or holiday events.	Belonging and present at all family events.
T. Leisure: walks dog independently around neighborhood, rides bike.	T. Increasing self-care; healthy living.	Seeking out and enjoying daily exercise.
T. First paid job in high school at Biggs Retail Grocery; works in produce department.	T. Has a purpose and makes contributions.	Training and support enabled Trent to have success at packaging and displaying the produce.
J. Wrote a grant with collaborating agencies: ACT Project (a statewide effort to prepare and establish employment for 8 adults with ASD).	J. Active in increasingly forming supports at the state level.	Project funded through state council on disabilities; coordinated the project; 8 adults with ASD received support and assistance.
T. Draws SSI.	J. Accesses governmental supports.	Helps offset T's living expenses.
J. Initiated guardianship.	J. New parental role; assists Trent in new ways when he needs help.	Legal guardianship established.
J. Applied for and received a leave from her job per the Family Leave Act in order to seek services for Trent.	J. Accesses governmental supports.	Received additional time to seek and access support and services for Trent's post-high school life.

Events	Choosing Beliefs and Principles	Outcome
T. Has 2nd job at Value Market. Biggs downsized and Trent and others were laid off.	T. Has purpose and makes contributions.	T. Works in produce and enjoys bagging candy and setting up displays.
T. Prom/graduation/party	T. Celebrates the ending of school and new beginning of adult phase.	T. After celebration ended, Trent stayed home, limited routine, much more time for TV watching.
T. Faced family issue. Brother has surgery for cancer.	T. Did not seem to respond to his brother's surgery.	Tumor was removed successfully.
J. Requests state emergency funds to hire a community coach. Trent has too much time doing nothing.	J. Seeks and accesses governmental resources to purchase supports.	T. Receives enough funding to hire a community coach for 12 hours a week.
J. Finds a person through a professional referral.	J. Seeks ways Trent can learn self-care and enjoy activities separate from parent.	T. Resists, but reluctantly agrees to participate.
J. Separates from Trent's dad. Trent exhibits depression; asks about dad.	J. I will help Trent and myself recognize and grieve for his losses.	J. Searches and finds a book (with cartoons) that explains divorce to a child in simple terms. No support with this topic found in any books related to disability.
T. Sees brothers less; they are attending college. Trent depressed and seems lethargic.	J. Will help Trent recognize and grieve for his losses (parental divorce, etc).	T. Social Stories™ and reading book on divorce and change help Trent somewhat.
J. Working full time at Kentucky Autism Training Center.	J. Will reach out to work collaboratively with other agencies.	T.'s depression, obsession increase slightly; stays more with his grandma when mom works. Too much empty time.
J. & T. move next door to J.'s brother.	J. Will reach out to others for assistance; I will seek to understand the benefit of change in my family's life.	J. Receives emotional and care giving support from brother and mother.

Events	Choosing Beliefs and Principles	Outcome
T. Job at Value Market worked very well. It is over because of the move to the other side of town.	J. Will allow Trent to recognize and have feelings about setbacks.	T. Leaves his job; he appears relieved and content.
J. Applies for Medicaid Waiver again; state lost application from 5 years prior. J. Applies for Community-Based Services that offers respite.	J. Seek and access governmental resource to purchase supports	Trent on waiting list for Medicaid Waiver. Trent receives respite through Community-Based Services; relieves Jackie and family members.
J. Tries to take Trent to several churches.	J. Believes people have a basic desire to be loved and accepted.	T. Obsesses in a Sunday School (difficult for teachers). Trent was not accepted.
J. Visits a church; seemed to have an open attitude; Jackie seeks a volunteer job for Trent and Bible class to attend.	J. Believes in the value that churches play in including people with disabilities.	A CLOSED DOOR Church does not respond to phone calls, Jackie's visits, or letters she wrote to minister.
J. Applies for the third year in row for Supported Living Grant. Each year denied.	J. Seeks a governmental resource to purchase supports; believes privileges and responsibility go hand and hand.	T.'s application is accepted. Jackie uses funding to purchase weekend community coach.
J. & T. have ongoing person-centered Planning meetings to find a job and establish other supports.	J. I will reach out to others for assistance negotiate a job; I will also value the team approach and their help in venues they can see as options and I can't.	J. & T. Monthly meetings to brainstorm and plan.
J. Hires another community coach on weekends to take Trent bowling and to their community activities.	T. Practices self-care; enjoys life.	David works well with Trent. Trent regresses still, but the option gets Trent out of the house. Trent obsesses with turning lights on and off (still has Virgil for community coach during week).

Events	Choosing Beliefs and Principles	Outcome
T. Exhibits increased obsessive behaviors.	J. Allow Trent to grieve; J. Seek support	T. David leaves, but makes suggestions for interventions for Trent.
J. Fires Virgil; he was always hours late. Hires Heather as a new community coach.	J. Practice self-care; And try to open new community experiences.	T. Trent appears to do better. He works out at the YMCA and goes out to eat, but still obsesses, but controllable.
T. Goes to camp.	J. Seek ways Trent will enjoy his life separate from his family.	T. Jackie is called to get him. Trent refused to do camp activities, he chose to stay at his bed.
J. A job is carved for Trent at YMCA, Person-centered planning helped. Barry and Troy with employment agency are offering supports.	J. Will seek help from others; Trent has purpose and can make contributions	T. For three weeks, Trent walks with a spring in his step. Loves his job, working in the laundry.
T. Begins to obsess at YMCA; Trent yells out when he was guided to the basement introduced to a new task, five minutes just before his shift ended. The job negotiations stated that he would have job coach assistance for new tasks learned.	J. Will allow Trent to recognize his setbacks and grieve his loss.	CLOSED DOOR Trent is terminated. We explained that he had likely had a time clock in his head and knew he was about to get off work.
Travis, Trent's brother, moves out of house.	Family structure changes, and Trent has to learn to adapt.	T. Grieves the absence of Travis.
J. Becomes unemployed.	J. Allow myself time to grieve my losses, Trent's adaptive difficulties.	J. Rests, replenishes herself; reflects about circumstance, reads to build and give back to herself; detaches from Trent and his issues. Applies for unemployment.
J. Divorced.	J. Will accept some relationships cannot be repaired or replaced. Recognize my loss and let go of previous hurts.	Closed Door. What is next?
J. Troy refers Jason, a friend, as a community coach to work with Trent.	J. Will seek and accept help from others.	J. Writes referral on note and stores in drawer, forgetting about it.

Events	Choosing Beliefs and Principles	Outcome
T. Heather, community coach stops working with Trent to go back to school; Jackie rehires Virgil to work with Trent again.	J. Not all decisions work out. I will allow myself to make mistakes on this journey.	Virgil is working with Trent.
T. Needs respite, Valerie provides service to Trent.	Establishing supports and hanging in there in the survival stage.	Valerie is wonderful and agrees to provide respite two days a week.
J. Buys new computer, writes action plan for consulting.	J. Takes steps to remain open and let go of a specific outcome.	Gives a talk at a conference (one that was already planned while having job at Kentucky Autism Training Center).
J. Accepts assisting a student and parent at an IEP meeting in Hardin County Schools; a student was a participant we had served in the ACT Project.	J. Takes steps to remain open and let go of a specific outcome, even when no motivation can be found.	J. Hired on the spot as a consultant three days a week.
J. & T. Trent's brother Travis has surgery for cancer again.	J. Takes steps to remain open and lets go of a specific outcome, even with little energy to give back to others.	J. Asks for work schedule for new job to be altered to stay with son one week out of three (during a span of 9 weeks)
T. Begins to obsess so severely, he focuses on items in store for nearly two hours and won't budge.	J. Recognizes that she can't be all to Trent; need help.	J. Stops taking Trent to store (used to be his favorite community errand).
J. Insists that Trent walk his dog once daily (the only productive activity daily).	J. Recognizes that she can't be all to Trent; we need help. I will seek help from others.	T. Trent now requires his uncle to come to house, help him out and into the car.
T. The only task Trent will accept is helping his grandma clip bushes and other yard work.	J. Recognizes that she can't be all to Trent; need help. Will seek help from others.	T. Helps Grandma several days a week in the yard.
J. Fires Virgil never to see him again.	J. Recognizes that sometimes bad decisions are made out of fear and desperation.	T. Has all free time within his week with no structure. This lasts about 4 months.

Events	Choosing Beliefs and Principles	Outcome
J. Troy again calls and refers Jason to Trent.	J. Accepts help from others.	Jason comes on Saturday and is Trent's community coach.
J. With person-centered planning carves a job for Trent at Papa John's; Trent folds boxes.	J. Will seek help from others; purpose and contributions.	Trent enjoys work. Works fast and stays on task.
J. Gets an invitation to go with college classmate to Panama.	J. Will give back to herself.	T. Uncle and Grandma and Jason on weekends cares for Trent for 10 days.
T. Trent obsesses and doesn't clean up well in the bathroom at Papa John's.	T. Will allow Trent to recognize his setbacks and grieve his loss.	T. Fired after 2.5 months.
J. Troy tells Jackie that Jason is looking for roommate and would live as Trent's assistant.	J. Takes steps to remain open, find courage and let go of a specific outcome.	J. Thinks about it, says no out of uncertainty. Then a friend encourages her to look at the pluses. Jackie agrees to try it out.
J. PCP supported living grant is rewritten, Seven County Services along with Community Employment, assists Jackie in asking for additional $$ in a grant requests for Supported Living.	J. Takes steps to remain open and let go of a specific outcome, with fear.	Trent is granted some additional $$$ to help him begin his new independent-assisted living.
J. Applies for Section 8 housing to reduce rent costs.	J. Takes steps to remain open and let go of a specific outcome, with fear.	Trent is approved.
J. Looks for an apartment.	J. Takes steps to remain open and let go of a specific outcome, with fear.	J. Moves out of the house she shared with Trent and Jason moves in.
T. Trent's first week living independently; goes to doctor for ingrown toe nail.	J. Takes steps to remain open, find courage, and let go for Trent to grieve his loss and accept his new life, with fear.	T. Obsesses 3 hours; Trent must be physically removed by Jason and uncle. (Trent is reacting to his new life without mom.)

Events	Choosing Beliefs and Principles	Outcome
J. Trent requires physical escorts from any community outing with Jason and Jackie.	J. Takes steps to remain open, find courage, and let go for Trent to grieve his loss and accept his new life, with fear and shame at times.	T. Jason, Trent's uncle, and Jackie patiently guide Trent and assure him that he is safe. His resistance lessens significantly after 3 months.
J. Jackie gets married.	T. Has purpose and contributes.	T. Participates in the wedding; escorts Jackie down aisle.
J. With the help of person-centered planning, negotiates a job for both Trent and Jason so Trent has Jason as a support when needed.	J. Believes in purpose and contribution. Trent keeps job for over one year.	Trent and Jason work in retail store in clothing, security tags. Trent successfully has that job for 15 months and enjoys working.

The purpose of the preceding pages was twofold: (a) to offer an example of the challenges that Trent and I faced that you may be able to relate to. Although circumstances may be different in many ways, these experiences are common among families with a member who has a disability. And (b) to illustrate that a person's beliefs and principles, whether conscious or unconscious, will guide decisions and actions.

Now It Is Your Turn — List Your Events, Choices, and Outcomes

Use the next few pages to reflect on the events, obstacles, and accomplishments the adolescent/young adult and your family have encountered. Determine the beliefs, values, and principles that guided your decisions. Pinpoint what actions and attitudes served as benefits for the young adult, as well as your family. This exercise can be extremely empowering as it can reveal your values and how the adolescent/young adult and/or the family did their best in a given situation.

Events	Choosing Beliefs and Principles	Outcome

Events	Choosing Beliefs and Principles	Outcome

Read the activities in this chapter and work through them at your own pace. It is alright if you do not do all of them. Completing just a few may help you recognize your perspective (i.e., your beliefs, principles, values) about your son/daughter or your family. The major changes involved in paving the way for an adult child's independence can be an emotional roller coaster for everyone in the family. To complicate matters, no one tells a family what to expect or how to handle the challenges along the way.

I have included plenty of examples from my personal life. Other parents who have lived through the process of guiding their young adult to independence have advice for you as well. This is what they want you to know about guiding your young adult to live in the community.

- "Keep an open mind. Don't put any barriers on anything. You never know who will be out there to be part of his or her life. It is a big change. Change can be hard and challenging, but it can be good. Don't rule out things "you think" he cannot do. I look back and recall saying, "Oh, he can't do that," but I was wrong.

- "It is all about finding the right agency. A lot of agencies are out there, and the family has to search for a good match, one that provides the services to meet the person's needs." The mother also talked about how her child was dependent upon support with facilitative communication. "If we had used one of the other agencies, we would have had to train the staff." And about employment, "Some agencies are better than others in finding jobs and matching those jobs to people."

- One mother recommended that if a family can get through all the difficult years and arrive at a better place for the individual and the family, that is real peace. "If I could do it, then anybody can."

- "Trust the young adult; give [him] a chance. Sometimes I think that [people see him] do things as not being as capable as he really is. I know what my son can [do]. People think that he can't do something, but deep down I know he can. He knows he can, too."

- "Families should not resort to placing their child or young adult on medication. It suppresses the symptoms. Parents can do things to eliminate the toxins in their child's body. Read Dr. Bernard Rimland's research and try the vitamin therapy. Parents have to get busy early to get their child healed."

- "Do it [preparing and exploring the community] over a period of time. You don't know what you can do unless you try. Don't settle for less than what you believe in your heart [for your young adult]. Start early. Don't assume brothers and sisters will take care of your young adult. They need their own life. You don't know who they will marry or if they move across the country because of their work. People with disabilities have a right to find their own life. They have a right to find their own life without me. Sarah has a good life."

- The parents both wanted their sons to live independently, and the dad learned to ask questions such as, "How much are we willing to risk? How much risk are you going to let happen?" The issue may not be whether the young adult is capable; it may be about the amount of risk taking parents are allowing their young adult to take.

- "They really need to know what their child is capable of doing. Have a real view of the setting that would work for your young adult. Do a lot of research."

- "Life is funny. I have Bill stories I share with families. It is possible to have pretty major difficulties and yet find your place. Be willing to work hard. That is the key to finding your place in this world. If you go [to] the wrong place or the [young adult] keeps getting hit in the head, it is going to kill [the young adult's] confidence. It is possible that a kid with a learning disability/ADHD can endure the death of a mom at a young age, or that a kid who has autism can end up living a life that is self-supporting. It can happen."

- "Tom is pleased with his life. He is successful. He has a great deal of pride. We have been so incredibly lucky as his parents. I would tell them they have to be their child's biggest advocate."

- "Start earlier than we did [the last year of high school] finding resources. The state's department of vocational rehabilitation won't even talk to you until your child is a senior in high school. There are big challenges in finding support services. Everything I found out was on my own. There isn't any book on how to prepare [your young adult] for college."

- "It is critical to network with other agencies and parents. Be active in searching for services and asking questions. Advocate for your child."

- "If [the] young adult has the desire and the interest, then he should be able to live independently."

It is sometimes easy to put your family's needs aside in order to be a caregiver, but remember that offering more than you have to give helps no one. As caregivers, it is important that we attend to our own needs, especially during crises or difficult times. It is my hope that these activities will help you determine what really matters in your family's life after you boil down all the issues and concerns surrounding the young adult's needs.

If you have already put considerable thought into this process, you have made giant steps toward self-empowerment. The circumstances you are facing today do not have to be your child's future, nor yours. Recognize that your best effort may look different from day to day, and that is alright. All we as parents can do is to try our very best.

CHAPTER FOUR
ROLES OF ADOLESCENTS AND YOUNG ADULTS

Identifying Strengths, Gifts, and Interests

"People with autism can create with full emotion in music or art that which they cannot show in relationships."
— Tony Attwood

The purpose of this chapter is to guide youth through a series of exercises to help discover what they enjoy, develop what they are good at, and learn more about their interests through hands-on experiences. Fulfillment of this lofty, yet realistic goal is dependent upon everyone recognizing that youth need something to do beyond filling up time with meaningless tasks and that youth must have experiences that lead to outcomes that cause them to give their best. Each individual has a name, a face, and a gift to offer that, when identified, can become valuable to others.

Some people with disabilities are living full lives and making a difference in the world. How did they reach this stage of living life fully with independence? You can read books about how people with ASD confront the challenges of living independently. A wonderful book, written by Zosia Zaks, *Life and love: Positive Strategies for Autistic Adults* (2006), offers everyday, practical strategies for living with independence in all areas of life. Zaks offers useful checklists and step-by-step approaches as a guide to navigating the community.

All the preceding chapters led up to the action-oriented tools presented in this chapter. Chapter One addressed the current situation for the majority of adults with disabilities and their families and the limited resources that often cause them to be isolated. Chapter Two offered strategies for professionals, in collaboration with the community and families, to initiate actions and projects that promote a youth's personal development. Chapter Three provided an approach for parent/family members to use to confront and handle the issues that often pose challenges during the transition phase. Together, these parties can build and secure a foundation that is required to create and drive a support system. It is essential that "supports," whatever they may look like, are established to make full inclusion a reality for persons with disabilities. In reality, the supports are all of us in the community.

To get started, we ask: How do young adults with ASD or DD find purpose and fulfillment in life? A person's gift or interest can be applied in various areas of living, whether as a hobby, entertainment, or paid employment. An example of employment includes a young man with autism who has a love for animals. One task that matches this interest may involve carving out a job to feed gerbils or birds, clean cages, or attend to the display and storage of animal care products. Many stores have pet departments. How do others benefit from his contribution? The store manager gains an employee who is perceived as valuable and as a team player, and who provides a worthwhile service. And society receives a contributing member who earns his own way, pays taxes, and becomes a consumer purchasing goods.

There are so many unmet needs in society and the world at large. People with disabilities can provide a service that meets some of those needs. It is a matter of matching the community's needs and the individual's gifts or interests.

Some may have tried to locate a job or hobby only to find a closed door. This is to be expected. Everyone who sets out on this path will inevitably face some rejection. But don't give up. Keep brainstorming and drawing support from the people who are able to help. Keep a positive outlook. Be assured that there is a place, person, or group who will be more welcoming and appreciative.

The following activities, if pursued and supported through an exploration process, can guide youth to learn more about themselves and what they can offer. The activities are designed to support the emotional growth of the individual as well.

Start by examining the positive effects of using a strength or gift.

A person's strength or gift can:

- be as powerful as any therapy, drug alternative, or medicine

- become the fuel that launches him into joy, delight, and purpose

- be the medicine that heals or lessens the challenges of ASD

- connect a person to associations and friendships because that is what a gift does

- take her to new heights and purpose while affirming value to the world

- produce positive outcomes in others, such as enjoyment or a lift in mood

- be empowering to and give hope for others to get through challenges

- reveal the essence of a person's personality and purpose during the act of doing or self-expression. When emphasizing gifts, the focus is shifted away from the label of autism or disability. When people notice the person's gift, they are noticing his capability, not the limitations of the disability.

School personnel write and teach students according to IEP goals and behavior management plans. Why not include a Gifts and Talents Action Plan (GTAP) in the educational program?

Youth need more than behavior plans. The GTAP is a plan to identify and explore the strengths and gifts for a student or young adult. The GTAP is a plan you will create in this chapter to identify and explore strengths and gifts. The process is exploratory and is quite different from setting goals and writing objectives for the IEP. The GTAP requires the support team to guide the individual to creatively try new experiences in order to discover interests or strengths.

Becoming Remarkably Able

The letters in the major part of the title of this book refer to actions that are encouraged in the activities of this chapter.

R Take positive **risks** to learn or try something new, even when failure is possible.

E Set goals and **explore** opportunities to reach them.

M Seek and find a **mentor** to guide and give you positive feedback.

A Participate in **activities** that have meaning and purpose (e.g., volunteer in clubs, church).

R **Resist** thoughts of failure and instead think "Yes, I can."

K **Keep** on walking your path, each day initiating at least one small action toward your goal.

A **Appreciate** and celebrate **all** successes, small and large.

B Set **boundaries** and let go of people or things that leave you feeling bad.

L **Listen** to your heart (the voice inside that encourages you). **Listen** to suggestions offered by people who care about you.

Y Seek organized programs for **youth** or community members where you can contribute to a cause that makes you feel accepted and good about yourself.

A **Affirm** your choice to give your best effort and express the real you.

B **Believe** you can move past a difficult experience and accept help from someone else.

L **Live** on purpose and know you *can* have a life where you are accepted and your gifts and strengths are valuable to others.

E **Expect** to fail; it happens to everyone sooner or later. Just get up, start again, and **ease** into your next try.

Below are definitions of terms used throughout this book. You may choose to refer to them as you do the activities or acting as a guide for the student completing them more or less independently. Some of them may merge, making it difficult to know the difference between a skill or talent. Don't be overly concerned about that. The goal is to find out what it the individual enjoys and is good at doing.

A gift — something a person is born with. It's something that comes as easy as breathing.

A talent — a gift the individual has pursued, developed, and refined.

A skill — something one learns to do. It may draw upon a person's gifts.

An interest — something that draws one's attention.

An experience — an emotional or mental perception that a person has or something physical that h/she has done (1997, p. 3).

Strengths — usually more voluntary than gifts and talents. Possessing a strength involves choices about when to use it and whether to keep building upon it. For example, telling the cashier that he undercharged you $5.00 shows personal strength and a decision to apply it. Thus, strengths can be built upon with time and effort (Seligman, 2005a).

Value — something of substance and/or merit; connected to a person's strengths.

Challenge — the hardest part of doing something, or trying something new.

Application — an awareness or action that can be attributed to or found beneficial for another area.

Inventory focus — a series of questions that lead in a particular direction, or to the next step.

Action — a way of doing something; making an attempt toward a goal, making headway.

Gifts and Talents Action Plan (GTAP) — a plan to help guide the process of exploring and identifying gifts, strength, and interests.

Discovering a Gift

After Trent had successfully been living independently for a year, I could see he needed something more to do, such as an interest or a hobby. He already had a job that was working out fine, but there was a void in his life; he needed an enjoyable activity to engage in in his spare time. I remembered back to Trent's school days and his teachers telling me that he liked working with his hands in arts and crafts projects. In particular, one of his inclusion courses in middle school was an art class, and the teacher commented that Trent participated well and really enjoyed the art projects.

I had just published my book *Independence Bound* (2001) and wanted to include Trent in my book signings. One way he could participate would be to make and give away bookmarks. I placed an ad for an art facilitator on a bulletin board at a local art store and received a phone call from a University of Louisville art student the very next day. That is how Trent got started in art. He enjoyed painting so much that I continued having Teresa, his art facilitator, come to his house weekly. After a few months, his paintings began to reveal a real gift.

As I think about how I was drawn to explore art with Trent, it becomes apparent that it was mainly by recalling what his teachers had said about his interests. He may always have had the gift, but I did not recognize it enough to explore it during his school years. Now his gift has opened up so much in his life and so much to others who enjoy his art.

When you are helping an individual explore his interests from the tiniest idea to the grandest scheme, ask what makes his flame inside burn. Tune into messages. They do exist. Listen carefully!

*"When you are completely caught up in something,
you become oblivious to things around you,
or to the passage of time. It is this absorption in
what you are doing that frees your unconscious
and releases your creative imagination."*

– Rollo May

Identifying Gifts and Strengths — Three Levels

Before starting the process of identifying and exploring gifts and interests, let's look at three levels of this process. The first level is obvious — it is apparent that the person has a gift, like a beautiful singing voice. The second level is easy to determine as well; this is when the individual indicates and directs her attention toward a particular area of interest, such as collecting stamps. The concern here may be to decide how this interest connects her to a hobby, employment options, and other people.

Finally, the third level is the most difficult because here advocates do not notice a gift or an interest as demonstrated by the individual. This is where the following activities come in. Stay focused on the idea that the actions to be explored are worth the effort. Be ready and open to an interesting and sometimes exciting adventure, disappointment, insights and, most of all, leave room for surprise.

Three Levels

1. The gift or talent is noticeable; for instance, playing the piano. It includes something you see, hear, or observe the individual doing; yet, he or she may need time and help in exploring how to use it.

2. The interest is evident; you can see something a person is drawn to but may have no idea how to develop that interest into a skill, a hobby, or a job. For example, attending to plants in the yard could develop into a job at a nursery.

3. No interests or gifts are noticed when observing the individual. The person does not have many interests that you see as useful. Here you have to look narrowly, seek a characteristic that is positive, something that is calming to the individual. Look for objects, environments, and people that work in the adolescent's favor.

This chapter offers assessments and activities that promote personal growth and independence. The assessments are categorized into two groups.

Part A: Activities for Persons Who Can Work Independently. These are for young adults who can read, explore, and make their own decisions. Somebody who is considered high functioning may be able to read this book independently, think and write about responses, as well as initiate some actions.

Part B: Activities for Persons Who Need More Assistance. These are for young adults who need an advocate or assistant to help them identify and explore gifts, strengths, and opportunities. This section may benefit persons who have mild, moderate, and sometimes severe disabilities.

All persons — regardless of the level of disability — can benefit from these exercises. Determine which section you need to read. Take your time, have fun and enjoy the process!

Part A:
Activities for Young Adults
Who Can Work Independently

Activity A-4.1 — Guiding Questions to Get Started

1. Is there something that would get you excited about each new day? If so, what would it be?

   _____

2. What can you do well? Or what could you do well if you had time to practice and learn?

   _____

   _____

3. What is your interest? _____

   Your passion? _____

4. If you could wipe away all fears and anxiety about your future, what dreams do you have?

   _____

5. If you could only do one thing with your life, what would that be? _____

   _____

6. Do you lose track of time when involved in an activity or interest? _____

   If so, which one? _____

7. Do you love the challenge of figuring out the solution to a problem? Give an example.

   _____

8. Are you curious about a specific thing? If so, what?

   _____

9. When you have a choice between something to learn or being entertained, how often do you choose the learning experience? _____

   How often do you choose the entertaining experience? _____

10. Do you pursue an interest or a particular activity beyond the time others might spend?

    _____

11. Do you delight in learning something specific? If so, give examples.

    _____

    _____

Activity A-4.2 — Tune into Messages That Reveal Gifts or Interests

Write any insights you may have noticed from past experiences. Remember this is an exploratory process, and you are a unique individual. Every number below may not reveal an insight to write down. That is O.K. Insights might come from the following:

1. A story you read or heard, or a movie that spoke to or inspired you or that left you feeling you want to do something that is a benefit for someone else

    _____

    _____

    _____

2. A place that someone mentions that may peak your interest

    _____

    _____

    _____

3. A hobby or activity that someone else has done that attracts your attention with a bit of energy and excitement

    _____

    _____

    _____

4.   An idea of interest that makes you stop, think, and imagine

_____

_____

_____

5.   Your reaction to events in your life

_____

_____

_____

6.   An environment or setting that seems to draw your interest

_____

_____

_____

7.   Associates from the past or present who had characteristics or personalities that brought out the best in you

_____

_____

_____

Activity A-4.3 — Consider Ideas Discovered from These Categories

Below are areas where gifts, skills, or interests may be found. Read through them to start thinking about what you might enjoy or want to do. Get a piece of paper and list the ideas that come to mind.

Listening:
- Do you like listening to stories?
- Do you show others how much you enjoy their company by giving them attention?
- Do you enjoy listening and participating with a group of people who are working toward a common goal (e.g., Sunday School class, environmental group, or planning committee for a fund-raising task)?

Showing someone how to do a task:
- Do you know how to complete a particular task, such as prepare a meal?
  If not, can you assist someone and then show them the steps?
- Can you show another person how to fix hair, put on makeup, arrange flowers, water and care for plants, put oil in a car, or wash a car?

Reading:
- Can you read about what interests you?
- Are you interested in going to the library?
- Can you use the computer to look up a topic of interest on the Internet?
- Do you read and learn new words that help you get around the neighborhood or help you with errands?

Writing:
- Do you make lists?
- Can you take a phone message and write down a phone number?
- Do you have an email address?
- Can you read email?
  If the words are too hard, can someone help you read email?
- Do you want to make a new friend and talk through email? (you may want to get help with this)

Computer:
- Do you know how to enter data into the computer or design graphics? Are you interested in exploring these areas? If so, ask your teacher or parent to help you find ways to use these skills.

Painting/crafts:

- Do you like to paint, mold clay, whittle wood, or sculpt?
  If you haven't tried it, do you think you would like to take a class at a local art store, or an adult learning class?
  You may want to ask someone to go with you.

Being still:

- Do you like to watch birds?
- Do you like to observe animals and their behaviors and responses?

Scientists make new discoveries by sitting quietly and watching behaviors. Scientists discover ways animals can help humans. Watching animals helps all of us learn about them. If you want to explore this area, you might visit the zoo and just sit and watch the animals. Appreciating how animals play, find food, and care for their young can lead you to learn more. The next step may be to see if you want to learn more about animals. If not, just sitting can be calming and relaxing.

Approaching a task with willingness:

- Are you open to learning something new?
- Can you try a new skill or task and look only at your willingness to learn? If so, you are successful.

At first, just let go of how well you do the task. Getting past the first step opens the door to learning more about how to do the task, one step at a time. So often measuring "willingness" to explore a task is not recognized as a valid positive effort toward success.

Organizing or categorizing items:

- Do you like to see items or objects in a certain order?
- Can you arrange things, such as your clothes in a closet, tools in the garage, or cartons in the refrigerator?
  If you enjoy this, explore ways to find a job organizing or arranging.

Sports:

- Do you enjoy a specific sport?
  If so, what kind?
- Can you find a team or a fan club to join?
  Or be a spectator for your favorite team?

Exercise:

- Is there a gym you can join?
- What kind of exercise do you like?
- What kind of exercise would you like to try?
- Would you like to join a nature hike club?

Enjoying your favorite music:

- What music do you enjoy?
- Do you play music in your room alone or with others?
- Have you gone to a concert?
  If so, what group do you like?
- Do you play an instrument? If so, what kind?
  Would you like to take lessons to improve your skill in playing the instrument?
- How can you share your favorite music with others?
- Is there a fan club to join?

Singing:

- Do you sing?
- Do you have a favorite singer or group?
  What kind of music do you like or does the group you enjoy sing?
- Can you find a choir or group to join (e.g., church choir)?

Dancing:

- Do you like to dance?
- What kind of dancing?
- Can you find a club or a class where you can take dancing lessons? Dance with others, meet new people?

Participating in an audience:

- Do you like to watch others sing and dance?
- Can you find festivals or community events where you can go and enjoy the entertainment?

Remember entertainers need an audience in order to express their gifts. The person sitting in the audience and appreciating the performance becomes a gift to the entertainer. These are ways that you can participate and enjoy being part of an event.

Activity A-4.4 — Make a Commitment

Write an agreement with yourself and commit to the exploration process. By accepting this first step, you have already started walking your own path to becoming *remarkably able*. Feel free to use ideas in this agreement or write your very own on another sheet of paper. The idea is to make a commitment to yourself.

A Sample Contract with Yourself

I,_____(your name), accept that I am walking my path to seek my strength or gift, who I can become, and how I can live my life.

1. I may or may not know my skills, strengths, or gifts, but I am willing to search for and develop them. I can list them in any way that is best for me; for example, write in a journal, tape record my thoughts, draw, paint, build a model, or cut pictures for a collage representing my interests and dreams.

2. When I think of a new idea or someone points an idea out to me, I am willing to ask for help or let someone show me how to try one of my skill(s), my gifts(s), my talents(s) in a useful way.

3. I will practice a new action of self-reliance (helping myself) or independence every day even if I need another person to assist or guide me.

4. I am open to try a new activity that may help me meet new people or learn a new skill. My skills may be useful in leisure activities or having a job.

5. I accept that when I try something new, obstacles will likely appear. Obstacles may bring out strong emotions in me. I give myself permission to feel and talk to someone I trust about how I am feeling.

6. I agree to find ways to take care of myself; sleep, eat healthy, and exercise.

7. I am willing to keep exploring how to develop new skills or use my gifts, even if they seem minor, or others laugh or think I am silly.

8. I give myself permission not to expect too much to happen at once, especially when it may look like I am struggling. I am succeeding because I have not stopped trying.

_____

signed   date

Activity A-4.5 — Gifts and Talents Action Plan (GTAP)

1. My goal is to guide myself to discover my strengths:

   _____

2. I will have achieved this by_____(date)

3. I know I will have achieved it because I will

   _____

   and feel

   _____

   or be able to

   _____

Here is an example of how the G-TAP works.

1. My goal in guiding myself to discover my strengths:
   I will participate in two new activities.

2. I will have achieved this by
   Next month

3. I know I will have achieved it because:
   I will keep a journal or a list of things I liked about the activities and the areas I may be fearful or resistant to in these activities.

   I will feel good about and reward myself for taking an action step toward walking my path to finding my gift.

Activity A-4.6 — Imagine Your Future

Using the ideas listed below, picture in your imagination how you would like your life to be. The purpose is to explore *how* you choose your life to be, not *what* you want to do. Often teachers or counselors ask students to think about a career or job when high school ends. You may have had an idea such as being a computer technician or a librarian, or you may not have any idea at all. Choosing a career is important, but other factors must be considered, too. In other words, imagining a job or career is not the purpose of this task. Instead, this activity encourages you to examine those things that reflect your preferences, your learning styles, and comfort levels around different people and environments. It is an opportunity to look within you and allow the learning styles and areas of strengths be considered as well. List:

Things you will have.

_____

_____

_____

_____

People in your life now and in the future (e.g., friends, coworkers — the people in your new life may be someone you have not yet met).

_____

_____

_____

_____

Where you are living. What do the surroundings look like — in the city bustling with people or on a quiet street?

_____

_____

_____

_____

Do you picture yourself working with your hands or your body?

_____

_____

_____

_____

What kind of work will you be doing? What skills are you using?

_____

_____

_____

_____

What kinds of products or services do you see yourself working around?

_____

_____

_____

_____

What level of responsibility do you envision yourself having and why?

_____

_____

_____

_____

What is the rhythm of your day? (examples: slow and easy, quick pace, relaxed)

_____

_____

_____

_____

What hobbies and other interests do you see yourself pursuing?

_____

_____

_____

_____

What kinds of help do you want to offer to others?

_____

_____

_____

_____

There is value in taking this as the first step toward establishing your life.

Activity A-4.7 — Just for Fun, Pretend

Imagine that you had three other lives to live. What would you do in your other lives? Some choices may include being a nurse, a ballerina, a singer, a computer wizard, a marine biologist, an author, a painter, an actress, a teacher, a fisherman, or a farmer.

Below, write a paragraph or story (or draw or paint a picture) about what you are doing in each of these lives. Next reread your story to someone or hang your drawing in your room. Find something you can do to act upon one of your stories. For example, if you want to be a singer, do you sing? If so, maybe you try out for the church choir.

Activity A-4.8 — Create a Collage

Collect brochures, photos, advertisements, and descriptions of what you dream to be or have in your life. Display your collage in your room to reinforce your dream. You can also bring your collage to a team meeting with people who want to help you. Show others what your interests and hopes are for the future. When you tell others about your dreams, you are becoming self-determined and your own best advocate. Congratulations!

Activity A-4.9 — What Is Positive and Useful About Your Skills and Gifts?

You may have a skill or gift, but may think that it could never be useful. Don't be so quick to toss it aside. Your skill may be as simple as making great coffee or a tasty deli sandwich. Nearly all tasks can be directly related to a job where you could use your skill to earn money. Talk to the people who listen to you and care about helping you. This may include your person-centered planning team friend or mentor to brainstorm an option for employment, leisure, service, or hobby.

List all the positive and useful things you can think about for some of these skills and gifts. For example, caring for a pet involves taking your dog for a walk, playing ball, feeding, bathing, petting, and teaching your dog tricks. Some of these tasks in combination could be a service you offer to neighbors or friends.

Some examples will get you thinking about where to search for your skills and interests. Go ahead and list all the useful tasks in each of these areas.

- Enjoying activities out-of-doors _____

   _____

- Cooking or baking _____

   _____

- Shopping at the grocery store_____

   _____

- Church activities _____

   _____

- Gardening _____

   _____

- Riding a bike_____

   _____

- Computer games _____

   _____

- An unusual thing you can do that no few can do (for example, whistle) _____

   _____

- Taking something apart _____

   _____

- Arranging parts of something into a whole _____

   _____

Activity A-4.10 — Rating Your Skills

List below the skills you have. Then rate them by how much you enjoy them. Circle the top four or five. (Remember, a skill is something you learned to do. Skills can be gifts, too.)

Below list your skills in the numbered column and rate your skills based on your most favorite (10) and your least favorite (1).

List your skills	Rate your skills from 10-1
1. _____	_____
2. _____	_____
3. _____	_____
4. _____	_____
5. _____	_____
6. _____	_____
7. _____	_____
8. _____	_____
9. _____	_____
10. _____	_____

Activity A-4.11 — What Is One of Your Interests or Gifts?

This activity can include interests or gifts. A reminder: *An interest is something that draws your attention; a gift is something you are born with and something you do almost as easily as breathing.*

Choose an interest of yours and brainstorm the many ways you could use it. For example, Bobby has a passionate interest in trains. Look at how Bobby listed ways he could use his interest in trains. Also realize how these could connect Bobby to the community. The same goes for Carol, who has an interest in painting as described below. What could she do with that interest?

Examples of Lists of Interests

Bobby
1. Building train stations is fun.
2. There are people who have the same hobby.
3. Bobby can talk to others who are interested in the same hobby. He can hang out at the local hobby store around others who like trains.
4. He can read hobby magazines and find events related to this hobby.
5. He can show someone how to build parts of a train village.
6. Bobby can write about his hobby through email or on Internet sites.
7. He can find a paid job in a hobby store assembling train stations and villages.

Carol
1. Painting is fun.
2. She could use a paint brush to mix different colors of paint. Discovering new colors is nurturing and calming.
3. Using her paint brush to make different lines and using various mediums and textures is interesting to her.
4. It is fun to create interesting shapes and surfaces.
5. She can collaborate with other artists in art projects.
6. Painting around other people who are artists helps Carol make new friends. Her talent is appreciated by other artists as well.
7. She shares her art with others.
8. She can sell her paintings.
9. She can shake hands and meet new people at art fairs and disability conferences where her work is exhibited. She is learning how her art is a contribution that people enjoy and value. She receives positive feedback when people comment that her paintings are beautiful.

Get out a clean sheet of paper. After reading the above examples, choose an interest you have, then brainstorm ways to use it. When you finish one interest, start over with a different one. See how many different lists of interests you can come up with and ways to explore them.

Activity A-4.12 — Gifts, Interests, and Environment

This activity asks you to list your (a) gifts/skills or strengths, (b) interests, and (c) environments that you already enjoy and/or places you may want to experience. You can use information you already recorded in connection with any of the activities you have completed. The pictorial of clouds represents your highest hopes about your capabilities and interests.

An example, Gifts, Interests, and Environment Sheet (example) Activity A-4.12 is provided on the following page regarding how to complete the activity. You may want to review it before you do the activity on your own on page 103.

Activity A-4.12 — Gifts, Interests, and Environment Sheet (Example)

Gifts/skills or strengths I have

- Painting on my canvas
- Being a part of, being included in family activities, games, outings
- Listening to jazz, blues, classical music
- Helping my grandmother with some yard work; I like clipping bushes best
- Cooking and baking

Interests — things I enjoy or want to try

- Expressing myself more fully
- Shopping at the mall for NIKE shirts
- Horseback riding
- Travel
- Going to more sporting events
- Owning my own house
- Friends of my own

Environments (places) I enjoy or want to experience more often

- Being part of a church
- Going on a vacation with my family
- Eating in a nice restaurant
- Being in pleasant settings where pop music is played
- Colorful items and environments
- Places where I have several choices
- Places where people are willing to help and understand my needs

Activity A-4.12 — Gifts, Interests, and Environment Worksheet

Gifts/skills or strengths I have

Interests — things I enjoy or want to try

Environments (places) I enjoy or want to experience more often

Activity A-4.13 — Using Your Gifts

Now look how you can use your skills, gifts, and interests in places that you enjoy or want to try. You may want to refer to the example Dream Sheet on page 105 before you complete your own.

From the Gifts, Interests, and Environment sheet (A-4.12) that you just completed, find the gifts and skills you listed in the top-left cloud. Next, using the Dream Sheet, Activity A-4.13, take those same gifts and skills you listed and write one skill or gift in each of the five cloud headings. Think about each one, then list any and all the places where your skills and interests can be practiced or offered to an organization, club, or some other place in the community. You may be surprised to learn how several of your options can become a chance to meet new people, develop a hobby, volunteer, or even create a job.

You may want to ask your teachers or family members to help you brainstorm ideas for applying your skills and gifts. After you have completed this activity, show the results to your parents, teacher, or person-centered planning team. The ideas may be helpful in your educational planning.

Writing down your dreams might bring them into your reality some day.

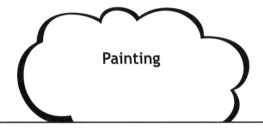

Activity A-4.13 — Dream Sheet (Example)

Painting

- Take art lessons at adult learning centers or art stores.
- Create with other artists in a studio.
- Paint and donate my art to clubs, churches.
- Sell my art at community festivals and events.
- Exhibit my art in local coffee shops.

Being a part of: spending time with my family and participating with others in a group

- Listen to and rock and blues bands.
- Get a job and assist a coworker at a job in the lawn dept.
- Watch a ballgame and participate in the chants.
- Visit art museums and collect books of famous artists and their paintings.
- Display my art at a disability conference.

Music: jazz, blues, classical

- Listen to the church choir.
- Sing in the church choir.
- Invite artist friends to cook out and play loud music.
- Attend community music festivals.

Outside: walking and yard work

- Walk my dog in the park daily.
- Paint a rug outside and give it to my grandma.
- Help my grandmother clip her bushes.
- Participate in an outside art festival selling my work.

Cooking and baking

- Paint the fruits and vegetables I like to cook and eat.
- Get a job in a coffee shop where art is displayed.
- Prepare a dinner with help and invite my family to an outside picnic.

Activity A-4.13 — My Dream Sheet

Activity A-4.14 — Look for Your Themes

Now look at your list from the prior activity and try to pick out themes.

Your responses are reflection of all the things that matter to you. This exploration could lead to a higher level of participation and active involvement in activities. You may also want to review the activities just completed in the pictorial clouds to answer the questions. Write your answers to the questions below.

Do you choose to work with your hands, use tools, plants, the earth, or other materials?

_____

_____

_____

Do you prefer to participate by yourself, with another person, or in a group of people?

_____

_____

_____

Did your list show that you prefer physical activity? If so, were you moving around in one environment by yourself or with other people?

_____

_____

_____

How does this activity benefit others or provide a service to help someone else?

_____

_____

_____

Does your list show that you are around people with whom you have a common interest? If so, what are those interests?

_____

_____

_____

Do you have an interest that could lead to learning a new skill? For example, if your interest is related to pets, what new training or skills could you learn?

_____

_____

Is that new skill useful or fun? Is it a service?

_____

_____

Can the new skill be used in daily living?

_____

_____

Do you see any opportunity where the skill or gift can eventually be a way to earn an income?

_____

_____

Is the skill or gift useful all year round or only at certain times of the year, for example, holidays?

_____

_____

Is the skill or gift useful for a particular season only; for example, summer?

_____

_____

_____

What themes were prevalent on your list?

_____

_____

_____

_____

Activity A-4.15 — You Say "I Can't"

Choose one thing from the themes activities (A-4.14) where you listed skills, gifts, or interests.

Now list some reasons you can't be, do, or have what you dream. That's right, just list why you can't and let's see what happens.

_____

_____

_____

_____

_____

_____

How do you know you can't have/do it? Who said so?

_____

_____

_____

_____

If someone told you that there is no way your interest or gift could be useful, ask the person to explain how she knows. Write your response showing you will continue pursuing the gift or interest. This is a way of advocating for yourself.

_____

_____

_____

_____

_____

_____

_____

_____

Meet Melissa

Melissa loves children and helps out in a day care program. Her goal is to work with the Red Cross or FEMA (Federal Emergency Management Assistance) to help people who have been struck by disasters. Melissa has overcome many challenges with autism, severe allergies, and blood clotting disorders. She was diagnosed as an infant with severe mental retardation, and her parents hoped that one day she would live in a group home setting. Her life has surpassed all predictions previously made by the experts. Indeed, Melissa has made tremendous growth, and through her own motivation and "with support," she has learned to live out the belief that "SHE CAN."

Activity A-4.16 — Now Say, "I Can"

Choose a skill you do well.

Now state all the ways you can express that skill.

_____

_____

_____

_____

_____

_____

How do you know you can do it? Who is encouraging you? You may be the only one encouraging yourself right now, and that is okay, but try to find someone who will listen to you and support your interest.

_____

_____

_____

_____

If someone is encouraging you to use your interest or gift, seek his or her ideas and knowledge about how you can use your gift/interest.

Activity A-4.17 — Building Your Self-Worth

List three people who have pointed out your positive traits or have encouraged you in some way. The person may have been your teacher, a neighbor, or your parent. Write what they said that was positive. Be specific. Even if you have doubts about the comment, write it any way. Their positive opinions may be true.

1. _____

   _____

   _____

   _____

2. _____

   _____

   _____

   _____

3. _____

   _____

   _____

   _____

Activity A-4.18 — More on Building Your Self-Worth

Think of someone from your past who doubted you. Recall and jot down what the person said, the details, and where it took place. Ask yourself, "How did I feel?" when this happened. Include what bothered you. For example, "I can remember when I was 11 years old and Aunt Sally gave me a goofy pat on my shoulder and started laughing when I told her that I wanted to be a teacher when I grow up." If you really want to be a teacher, explore the option. Going to college and getting through all the courses may be your goal.

If college is not for you, realize that there are many other ways to teach people. Schools need assistants in the classrooms in elementary and kindergarten. Other options include working in a day care program or a preschool Sunday school class. Ask your teacher, neighbor, or family member to help you explore. If you truly want to enter a particular career, there are many options and ways.

_____

_____

_____

_____

It helps to learn through other examples. Let me introduce you to Kirk.

Kirk

Throughout his school years, Kirk's teachers told him that he was not very good academically. He did not have many friends. Kirk had to face this negativity for a long time.

Kirk had limited opportunity during his school years to use his creativity. School assignments were too structured and rarely allowed his creative nature to emerge. Today at 21 years old, Kirk lives in his own apartment and is a gifted pianist. He plays beautiful classical and jazz music. He performs for elderly patients who live in a nursing home. His goal is to work in a nursing home doing other tasks, such as food preparation and/or care giving. His mother says one of his strengths is being nurturing to others.

Kirk's gifts:
- making others laugh or smile
- entertaining
- filling the recreation hall with beautiful piano music
- lifting people's spirits as they sing and dance to his music
- providing comfort and joy to people who may rarely see their family members

---

Activity A-4.19 — What If Failure Isn't Possible?

Write a paragraph or two about what you would do if you knew you couldn't fail. If writing isn't your preferred way of expressing yourself, use another media. You can voice record, draw a diagram, or paint a picture, if you prefer. Do what is ideal for you. If you are a young teenager, is it joining a choir, or playing an instrument you want? You may be 19 years old and leaving high school soon. Do you wish to have a job for 16 hours a week in the neighborhood grocery store? Do you want to live in your own apartment with a roommate or maybe by yourself? Suppose you want to learn to ride a horse, but you are worried that someone will laugh at you or you will fail somehow? No matter what your desire is, think success, and believe that failure is not possible. So what if the outcome does not appear as successful as you wanted, you are already a success by just trying.

Sarah

Sarah's community coach has introduced her to a variety of activities. She enjoys swimming laps, ice and roller skating, riding a 4-wheeler, and dancing at a local club with a support person. Sarah lives independently and is employed as an interdepartment mail deliverer at the county clerk's office, where her job coach provides some support. She has overcome many obstacles with sensory/behavioral issues and is considered very low functioning without her supports. Yet, Sarah has many gifts and interests and enjoys her independent life. "Others in the community see Sarah as a positive example of living life fully even with a disability," comments her mother.

Activity A-4.20 — Test Your Motivation

This activity suggests you take a step forward to increase your motivation. The activity builds your motivation to start or continue a project/activity. First read the two following examples of how famous people kept trying until they found success.

"Picasso created over 20,000 works of art, most of which were considered worthless. But he learned and sharpened his technique from each try."
— Ray Anthony and Malcom Kushner

"I think and think for months and years. Ninety-nine times, the conclusion is false. The hundredth time I am right."
— Albert Einstein

There may be a hobby, a skill, or an interest you would love to try but have not attempted because you lacked the motivation or support to get going. You may fear failure or fail to see that doing the task is worth the effort. Also, you may feel uneasy about entering a new setting where you do not know anyone.

These beliefs and fears are obstacles that can stop you from pursuing your interests. It is often necessary to participate in a group in order to use your gift or strength in a viable way. Here is a simple approach to help you. Test yourself. Do some basic steps first. If you pass your own test with these basic steps, success is guaranteed.

Consider this situation: Suppose you want to become involved in a group that helps protect our environment. You have found such a group in the new church you are attending. Think about how you can join the group when you do not know anyone.

Some suggestions include the following:

1) Call the minister and ask for an appointment to introduce yourself.

2) Tell him you are a new visitor to the church and that you would like to talk to someone about available programs/classes or volunteer projects in which you might be interested.

3) Ask a family member, neighbor, or friend to go with you if it makes you feel more comfortable. If you already know a member of the church, involving that person would make it much easier to get started.

4) Next, meet with the minister. It is likely the minister or his administrator will welcome you and introduce you to the director or chairperson of a class, volunteer committee, or project. That person will probably tell you when the next class meeting will take place.

5) On the day of the meeting, go a few minutes early. When you arrive, say hello to the person you previously met. That will make it easy to be introduced to others. You can also introduce yourself by just approaching someone to say "Hello, my name is_____"

6) Next, listen as a participant in the group. Think about the group's purpose and whether to volunteer or participate with others.

These steps represent the hardest part of inclusion and interacting, especially if you are shy or nervous. Consider a setting you might like to join. On a piece of paper, write down the steps you might initiate. If you try these first few steps, they reflect your strong motivation. Success *feels* great. When you succeed at helping yourself, the joy you feel is like nothing else. It will become easier each time you try something new.

Remember, if you need someone else to help you, that is O.K. Everyone needs some support at one time or another. Commit to trying this process in other areas until you have developed a confident attitude to help yourself. Keep trying until you achieve some progress. It may require many attempts to find where you want to spend your time and the people you have something in common with. This activity can help you build your motivation, capability, and self-determination as you approach a project/activity you want to learn or do.

George

I want to introduce you to George, a man in his 20s who has Asperger Syndrome. His story will reveal how motivation worked in his situation. Painting had been his joy for many years. According to his mother, "George's art was his entry into society. He is at his best when he is doing his art and conversing with people about it. He sees the world differently and wants to help solve its problems."

George was a member of his parents' church for a number of years. At the age of 24, he had a great interest in helping out with different projects at the church. He volunteered for every single committee and patiently waited for someone to call. After one year of no phone calls or contacts by the church committee members, he informed his parents that he wanted to find another church. He went down the street to the first church he found, walked in, and asked the minister, "If I come to your church will you let me volunteer?"

Today George is the very first person church members see as they walk through the door on Sunday morning. They are greeted with a handshake and a big smile. He is an example of how our youth and young adults show actions of motivation. George is a wonderful example of how just being willing to take the first step becomes motivating.

Activity A-4.21 — Revisit, Imagine Your Future

Now that you have worked through several exercises, you may have discovered a new dream. Write about your dream(s), what you want to become, and how you know when it has come true. Don't judge your dream as being silly or outlandish. Just write down your dream(s).

_____

_____

_____

_____

_____

_____

_____

_____

_____

_____

_____

_____

_____

Activity A-4.22 — How Setting a Goal Can Help

What is it that you want to make happen in your life this week, this month, this year, for the next five years?

This week:_____

_____

This month:_____

_____

This year: _____

_____

What problems do you want to solve? (for example, getting a driver's license, finding a job, developing a hobby)

_____

_____

_____

_____

_____

_____

What material things do you need or want to have? (for example, a guitar, car, computer, an apartment)

_____

_____

_____

_____

_____

What work or activities would you love to try?

_____

_____

_____

_____

_____

_____

_____

Activity A-4.23 — Turn All Your Desires and Dreams into a Goal

Below are some important ideas (Beattie, 1987, pp. 157-158) that can help you find your path and keep you focused on your goal. I found these ideas helpful.

- **When you have a problem, make solving it a goal.** What is it that you want, a new black leather jacket or a membership at the YMCA to work out? Turn it into a goal. Do you want to go some place — camping, shopping at the mall, seeing a concert starring your favorite entertainer? Do you want friendships, a club, or a place to belong? What are your interests? Turn making a decision into a goal. Do you want to lose weight, ride a bike regularly, or take a painting class? You can turn just about every part of your life into a goal. If something bothers you, make it a goal to fix it. If you want something, turn it into a goal.

- **Get rid of saying, "I have to."** Don't be tied down with all the "have-to's." You don't have to have a job a McDonald's just because all the people you know work there. If you cannot get rid of all the "I have to's," at least get rid of half of them.

- **Don't limit yourself.** Dream big and give your best effort to find solutions to your problems and achieving your dreams.

- **Write down your goals.** Power comes to those who write down goals rather than just loosely storing them in their minds. By writing your goals, you find focus and organization. I discovered that once I put my goals and dreams on paper, I actually released the outcome. I recognized I have done my part. Let go. Hang your goals on the refrigerator, in your bedroom, or on the bathroom mirror. Do what you can, one day at a time. Do what you can within the time frame of a day. Do what you are inspired to do.

- **Mark off the goals as you reach them.** As you work on your goals, notice the small steps of progress. This gives you confidence to keep going. Take time to congratulate yourself and celebrate. You can begin to see that good things do happen.

- **Be patient.** Trust that your goal will be solved at the right time. Don't ever say, "Oh, this problem will never go away. Or this dream will never come true." Your thinking is not true; your goal just hasn't been reached yet.

A goal I want to work on:

_____

_____

_____

_____

Activity A-4.24 — Recognizing People Who Support You

There are people who care about what you are learning and doing; that is, care about your well-being. There are also people who do not support you. If someone does not get along with you, it may be more about their own problems than it is about you.

Here is an activity to help you recognize people who are your allies, your supports, your friends. It is also about noticing those who are not helpful to you. It is common and normal for everyone at one time or anther to have to deal with people who are difficult. That is life. This activity will help you differentiate those who are helpful from those who you must tolerate.

On page 123, you will see a circle. Inside the circle, write down the names of people you need to answer to (parents, teachers, employer, yourself, etc.). Also put down names of people who are supportive of you and your interests (parents, friend, aunt, a teacher, etc.). The names you put inside the circle are the people you know are on your side. Outside the circle, place names of people who are not your best allies or represent your best interests. For example, you may put Sally's name on the outside of the circle because she is a girl who laughs at you. She may be a person whom you should not talk to about your dreams.

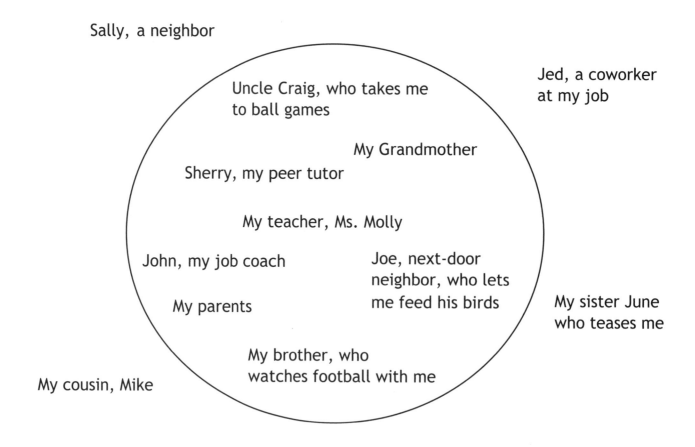

Sally, a neighbor

Jed, a coworker
at my job

Uncle Craig, who takes me
to ball games

My Grandmother

Sherry, my peer tutor

My teacher, Ms. Molly

John, my job coach

Joe, next-door
neighbor, who lets
me feed his birds

My parents

My sister June
who teases me

My brother, who
watches football with me

My cousin, Mike

Now it is your turn.

If someone is hurting you deliberately, do not tolerate their behavior. Seek help. Quickly tell someone you trust — a teacher, counselor, or neighbor. If you see your situation as extreme, call the police or go to an emergency clinic. This is your way of expressing self-care and strong self-determination, which is your right. Never tolerate abuse in any way.

Activity A-4.25 — Finding Time

You may say you don't have time for activities, such as homework or the hobby you want. It helps to look closer at how you are spending your time. Where does your time go? Below, list five major activities you did this past week. You might notice time to spare for a new activity, or you might schedule needed downtime or alone time.

1. _____

2. _____

3. _____

4. _____

5. _____

Think about the following questions.

How much time did you give to each one? _____

_____

Which activities were the ones you wanted to do? List activities where you are showing responsibility but that you may or may not enjoy (e.g., cleaning your room, doing laundry). Which activities promote your growth (e.g., doing homework, volunteering your time, or giving someone a helpful hand when he or she needed it)?

_____

_____

_____

_____

_____

How much time do you spend only on your own interests or for your personal benefit (for example, relaxation)?

_____

_____

_____

How much time you do spend helping others?

_____

_____

_____

Are there people around you who will help you find solutions to making changes that will benefit you or promote your personal growth? Ask for help and support.

_____

_____

_____

Activity A-4.26 — What Activities Do You Enjoy?

It is important to do things you enjoy, but sometimes it is easy to get into a rut and end up doing the same things over and over, even forgetting other activities you once enjoyed. List 10 things you like doing. Include activities that you have not done for a while; for example, walking your dog in the park, hanging out with friends, playing video games, baking cookies, making homemade soup, watching TV, riding your bike, painting, arranging flowers, shooting baskets, hiking, browsing through magazines, or reading books in the library or a book store.

Write down the date you recall doing the activities. You may be surprised to learn how long it has been since you last participated in the activity. After you make the list, think about which activities you want to do again. Consider what has to be done to participate again. The goal can be small, like getting your bike repaired so you can ride it. Remember, the idea is to have options and not get in a rut doing the same activities each day. You might recognize a skill or gift you have. Ask for help from others, if needed, and schedule time for some new and different activities.

Things You Enjoy Doing	Date You Last Did the Activity	Check the Activities You Want to Try Again
1. _____	_____	_____
2. _____	_____	_____
3. _____	_____	_____
4. _____	_____	_____
5. _____	_____	_____
6. _____	_____	_____
7. _____	_____	_____
8. _____	_____	_____
9. _____	_____	_____
10. _____	_____	_____

Activity A-4.27 — "Living Your Life" Pie

Take out a sheet of paper and draw a circle. This activity is about increasing your quality of life. Draw lines inside the circle, similar to slicing a pie. Write a label for each piece: exercise, play, work, school, friends/companions, family activities, and spirituality/church. You can choose other labels if you wish, these are just examples.

Next, place a star on each piece, indicating the extent to which you are satisfied with that area of your life. For example, place a star on the outer edge for family activities if you are very satisfied in this area. Place a star in the slice close to the inside of the circle called friends if you are hoping to have new friends (a girlfriend). That means you are not very satisfied with this area.

Now look at where all your stars are. If most of your stars are in the outer part of the circle, it means that you are very satisfied with most areas of your life. Notice the stars that are near the center of the circle and read what the piece is labeled. These areas may need some attention in order to increase your quality of life.

This exercise will show you areas where you need to focus your attention. You may want to seek assistance in increasing positive experiences in these areas.

Example

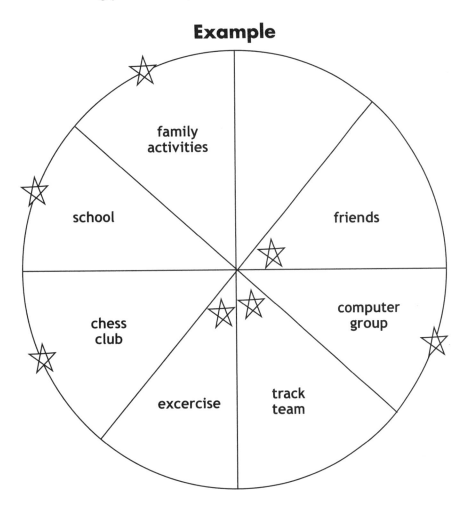

Activity A-4.28 — Choose a Positive Role Model

Who are your role models? Everybody has a role model. You may have to stop and think about it, though. Choose a person you have met, saw on TV or in a movie, or read about in a magazine, who has made a positive impact. The person could have accomplished something great or overcome an obstacle. The person(s) you choose may be famous now, someone who lived long ago, or a person you admire or respect in your school, church, or community. For example, you may choose someone you know, like the quarterback of your school's football team or the head cheerleader.

List one or several people you respect.

_____

_____

_____

What does the person do that you most admire? Choose one of the qualities you respect and practice it in your own life, if just for a day. Express what you learned from the full-day practice. Write about it, draw a picture about it, or just tell someone.

_____

_____

_____

_____

_____

_____

Susan

Introducing Susan: Susan has enjoyed music since she was a small child and has many role models who are singers in the entertainment field.

Susan says, "Life without music is unimaginable. If a life is a life without music, it's boring," Susan said. "I don't care what kind of music it is — I love it."

Susan takes music classes at the community college and lives in an apartment with a roommate. She has appeared on several national talk shows. Her mother said, "Susan is a compassionate young woman who wants to teach others about what it is like to live with a disability, Williams Syndrome."

Activity A-4.29 — The *Remarkably Able* College-Bound Student

Persons with disabilities may require additional support to successfully attend college. Supports may range from a particular technical device, to a learning strategy, or taking tests without time limits.

Independent living skills are usually taught in high school and encouraged as the young adult goes to college. These skills reveal what students are supposed to know and apply to help themselves. Unfortunately, that is usually not enough. When striving to function at higher levels, such as in college, students must also learn to let go or give up some comfortable preferred activities or habits:

- Decrease the length of time involved in preferred activities, (e.g., computer time)
- Give up sleeping late into the morning hours
- Give up a familiar routine and recreate a new schedule

So you want to go to college and earn a degree? Maybe you just want to take classes and figure out later what degree you will pursue. Having what you want requires working with persistence, but it also requires giving up some things you are used to doing.

The question becomes, What are you willing to give up in order to reach your goal? For example, are you willing to let go of the amount of time you now spend doing preferred activities. It is not suggested that you stop doing these preferred activities. They are important for relaxation between going to class and studying, but the time spent on them may be cut down.

Here is a basic how-to process. It is not an unfamiliar process. All of us have to go through this. Wanting to go to college and accomplishing it are two different things.

Jim

Jim wants to earn a degree in computer graphics. His goal is to work in the home office of a large pizza company in his home town. How can he move from his current position at a small sign shop to acquiring a career with a large company?

How can he reach his dream profession and yet start within his world as it is?
- He will trade in his full-time job for a part-time job in order to take college courses.
- He will abandon his days of sleeping late and hours watching TV to allow time for taking classes.
- He will budget his cash in order to pay for updated computer software that will be used to increase his expertise and skill in designing graphics. This may leave him without spare cash for movies.
- He will trade his nights out with friends for hours of study and preparing for class assignments.
- He will trade his defensive ego for resilience and courage when he faces customers who want to order a sign. Many of these customers are very controlling and direct about the final product they want. They may be unwilling to listen to what a professional who knows graphics might recommend. Doing the work may mean that Jim takes steps in his work to complete his tasks even if it limits his self-expression. That is typically what most of us have to do in our careers.

State a goal and list what you may need to give up to reach it. You may want to ask for assistance from someone who knows the steps to *your* goal.

_____

_____

_____

_____

_____

Examine your own qualities and list the ones that need improvement.

_____

_____

_____

_____

_____

_____

_____

List ways you can improve.

_____

_____

_____

_____

_____

Visit your list often and determine how well you are progressing. Keep working at it and choose another quality that needs your attention.

Important Qualities That Lead to Success in College

Positive attitude — Try to look at the best of every situation. If you get a low grade on a test, ask yourself what you can learn from it. Maybe you can have a tutor before the next test. Is it possible you did not study long enough or misunderstood the major sections in your notes you were supposed to study?

Commitment — Be willing to go to class and study every day. Are you late for classes or get lost often? What can help you, a loud alarm clock or written directions to your destination?

Daily satisfaction — Everyone gets frustrated. You may need to examine more closely the source of your frustration. If you are slipping behind academically, not getting to class on time, or not turning in important paperwork to the financial aid office, it may be a problem of organization. Don't blame others. Determine how you can organize these details better. Make a "to do" list for each simple task. Remember, do not hesitate to ask for help when you need it.

Balance — Be careful to schedule your day with a variety of activities. Are you getting enough sleep, physical exercise, and eating at least one good meal a day?

Feedback — This is tricky for many people. You may find out you misunderstood an assignment. Be willing to talk with your instructor or a fellow student and start your project all over again to get it right.

Independence — Being independent does not mean you cannot ask for help or rely on the advice from others. Expect as much independence from yourself as possible, but ask for assistance when in doubt. When you use problem-solving strategies to handle a situation, you are experiencing true growth and maturity. Just recognizing your effort is reinforcing. It keeps you focused and shows maturity and growth.

Understanding — Do you understand your own academic strengths and challenges? Can you convey that to yourself, to another?

Flexibility — Be willing to assess your strengths and weaknesses and modify your goals if necessary. For example, if you like the health care field but cannot make the grades to become a nurse, perhaps you can become a nurse's aide. Millions of nondisabled persons have used this strategy to find a career. The same approach can work for individuals with a developmental disability. Who knows, the nurse's aide might become the nurse later on.

Recognize Your Strengths and Challenges

Consider the follow questions. The answers can help you recognize what choices you have that promote success.

Do you prefer a smaller college campus with small class sizes? _____

_____

Do you prefer quiet environments to study? _____

_____

Do you understand explanations better when listening or when reading? _____

_____

Do you find that drawing models or diagrams helps you understand a difficult concept?

_____

Do you need to have freedom to move to different settings in order to focus and study?

_____

Do you prefer one specific place to study, such as your room or dorm? _____

_____

Do you understand an idea better when another person does it first, showing you each step?

_____

Do you need extra time to read class assignments? _____

Take notes? _____ Study for tests? _____

Do you benefit from frequent breaks during study time in order to stay focused on the material?

_____

_____

If you are still in high school and preparing for college next year, have you:
- taken the ACT, SAT, or other entry tests? _____
- arranged a time to register for a tour at the school you are considering attending?
  _____
- written a list of questions to ask a counselor at the college? _____

Some of the areas to ask about when you visit a college include:

- tuition _____

- student grants and loans_____

- foreign language requirements _____

- number of credits required to complete an academic program_____

- campus dorms or apartment information _____

- clubs to join and activities that are interesting _____

- disability departments and the information they provide to students _____

You should be able to describe well any difficulty you might have with getting to classes, preparing and/or studying for classes, joining clubs to develop friendships, and so on. Ask what help is available in these areas.

- Procedures and rules for receiving assistance through the disability department. What are the deadlines for applications?

- Accommodations for test taking. Remember it is your responsibility to ask questions until you understand them. If you request a service, know that it is your responsibility to follow through with the steps to receive it.

- Requirements such as letters of recommendation or entrance exams to submit to the advising counselor.

Develop Friendships at College

Investigate the following options, because they can lead to meeting new people and possibly developing friendships.

- Part-time work study

- Study groups with other students

- Campuswide events where students and professors participate or meet

- Tutors or mentors to assist you

Activity A-4.30 — Personal Growth Outcomes

Other young adults have made positive changes in their lives. Their outcomes are noted below. If you have completed some of the activities in this section, you are on y our way to discovering possible ways to use your talents and strengths. An increased quality of life is sure to follow if you keep working on identifying and using y our strengths and gifts.

R   **raised group consciousness** through self-expression and contributions

E   **emotional** growth

M   **matured** through confronting challenges

A   knows and enjoys **acceptance** among others

R   takes **responsibility** for him/herself and others

K   gained **knowledge** of his/her own limitations and capabilities

A   **appreciates** his/her place in life

B   participates as an owner in own **business**

L   **lives** in and is purchasing a home

Y   became a compassionate **young** adult teaching others through personal expression (e.g., singing, performing, and/or offering insights so others can know how to support and respect people who have ASD and other disabilities)

A   **appeared** and performed in entertainment venues, media, weddings, art exhibitions

B   created and painted **beautiful** pieces of art that allowed the artist to compete with other well known artists and win honors

L   enjoys **living** his or her own life

E   **employed** in a work that matches his or her skills and gifts

My interviews with parents about how young adults with ASD were capable of full community living have revealed one significant impact that brought success to each young adult — developing his or her self-expression by applying a gift, a strength, or a strong interest to an area that offered employment, leisure, or a connection to the community and to others.
Some of the young adults' gifts included:
- painting with acrylics
- playing classical music on the piano
- memorizing and analyzing various sports statistics
- excelling in bookkeeping skills
- strong interest in animated technology
- teaching parents and people with ASD how to use facilitated communication tools
- strong geographical knowledge and application
- caregiver — nurturing toward elderly and small children

Activity A-4.31 — Creating your MAP, MY ACTION PLAN

The Steps

WOW!! Now that you have spent a great deal of effort toward exploring gifts, strengths, talents, and interests, it is time to develop your personal MAP (My Action Plan). Have handy the answers to the activities you already completed. You will want to include in the vision, beliefs, principles, and goals the information you learned about your interests and gifts. If you choose, invite others to help you: a family member, a neighbor, someone who knows you well.

1. **Start writing the highest vision you have for yourself.** Use the MAP sheets (pages 138-141) right after the Map example. Remember, a vision is a clear image of your future.

2. **Select one or more of your beliefs.** The belief(s) should reflect your concept of the highest attainable life you see for yourself.

3. **Write down your principle(s).** Make sure the principle you selected is supported by one or more of your beliefs. Without that provision, you cannot live by your principles. Your principle starts with "I will." You can review the activities, especially Activity A-4.6 to determine your principles.

4. **Decide on specific goals.** There may be several, but you should list at least two. Some areas you may want to reflect in your goals can be found from Activity A-4.27 — Living Your Life Pie. Include exercise, play, work, school, friends/companions, family activities, and spirituality/church.

5. **Determine the activities necessary to achieve the goals you have set.** You may find that you will need to break each activity into smaller ones until you can complete each of them.

6. **The final step is to design an ideal weekly activity schedule.** Update this list often and have it in view so you can look at it until you have reached your goal(s).

Review and readjust the activities monthly. This process is about moving forward until the goal is reached. Before you start writing your plan, review the example provided.

Johnny

My Vision

I see myself living in my apartment off Frankfort Ave. I like this area because I can walk to restaurants, shop, and go to coffee shops where I can hang out. I love my part-time job working around musicians in a place where my knowledge of a variety of genres, especially classical music, is appreciated. I am learning to play the guitar. Most of my associations and friends are centered around my music interests.

Johnny's Belief List

I know I can live in my own apartment. I believe the best place for me to live is on Frankfort Ave where there are small retail stores, restaurants, coffee shops, and a bus line. I love music, and small bands play on the sidewalks on Frankfort Ave and nearby parks during the summer. I believe I can share what I like and know about music with other people. I believe I can learn how to play the guitar, too.

Johnny's Gifts

A principle Johnny is working toward:

I will accept responsibility and guidance from those who want to help me achieve my goals.

Personal Challenges
(with parental or advocate assistance)

Johnny has Asperger Syndrome and find it difficult to interpret others' viewpoints as well as understand the cause and effect of his responses or actions.

Funding to hire agency, support person, mentor to:

- Offer frequent follow-up on independent living skills and activities
- Develop checklists to follow a schedule
- Assistance in finding employment

Goals

Parent/advocate will help:

- Find an apartment for son near bus line and off Frankfort Ave within one year after graduation
- Seek agency/or hire someone person to offer support (frequent check-in)
- Create a financial plan of support
- Help plan a daily or weekly schedule to give Johnny some structure to work with

---

Johnny's Commitment to the Goals

I will:

- Accept help from my support (parents, professionals, etc.) for employment and finding an apartment
- Be responsible for personal care, cleaning room/apartment
- Seek employment
- Receive help in finding and maintaining a job
- Show willingness to keep checklists and schedules
- Take guitar lessons

Parent and Young Adult Activities (Example)

Apartment:
- Check for information about HUD housing rentals.
- Get agent to help find apartment.
- Shop for furniture in second-hand stores.

Seek Support:
- Make appointments and phone calls to agencies.
- Find a mentor or community coach.
- Inquire from agencies about services or assistants who are available to provide support (frequent check-in) even if it is private pay.
- Invite people the young adult met during the exploration activities.

Seek Employment:
- Seek a contact name to inquire about work tasks for a job at a talent agency.
- Seek possible part-time job at a music store where CDs are sold.
- Seek employment agency on disability to find a job.
- Seek supports through Vocational Rehabilitation.
- Inquire about self-employment, starting business in area of interest of music (i.e., bring CDs to nursing home during recreation and offer a brief history of the composer and play the pieces).

Create a Financial Plan of Support:
- Seek information and determine SSI or SSDI income eligibility.
- Inquire about a special needs trust fund.
- Obtain information on life insurance.
- Anticipate possibility for individual to earn income from employment.

Network:
- Make list of people and invite them to participate in a person-centered-planning team meeting to explore ideas for employment and hiring support person.
- Invite music director of the church where the family attends to participate in team planning. Also inquire about teaching John guitar lessons.
- Invite people the young adult met during the exploration activities to help brainstorm for employment or leisure in knowledge and appreciation of classical music.
- Invite case service representative at a local mental health agency.
- Invite a representative from an autism or Asperger support group.

MY ACTION PLAN
(MAP)

A vision is a clear image of the future which is attainable.

My Vision

_____

_____

_____

_____

_____

Beliefs refer to why we live our life.

My Belief

_____

_____

_____

_____

Principles refer to how we live our life.

My Principle(s)

_____

_____

_____

_____

_____

My Challenges

_____

_____

_____

_____

Goal One

_____

_____

_____

_____

Activities

_____

_____

_____

_____

_____

_____

_____

_____

Goal Two

_____

_____

_____

_____

Activities

_____

_____

_____

_____

_____

_____

_____

_____

_____

Goal Three

_____

_____

_____

_____

Activities

_____

_____

_____

_____

_____

_____

_____

_____

_____

_____

Do not give up. Keep moving through this process. You never know when something or someone will become a solution to living your life more completely. Some ideas may include assistance or meeting new people who can help you in school, find a job, or live more independently.

Part B:

Activities for Young Adults Who
Need More Assistance

The purpose of this section is to provide further explanation to the parent, advocate, or assistant who will be initiating the activities with a student or young adult who needs support to do the activities. All activities are numbered to match Part A. Do not skip reading Part A. As you walk the student through an activity in Part B, you may want to refer to Part A.

Some of the activities may require more than one person's opinion about the student's interest, strength, or gift. A team approach is most helpful. For example, school personnel may see different capabilities than parents, and vice versa. Remember that the premise here is that when the young adult's daily life is built using his or her gifts, strengths, and interests, capability and involvement increase.

Activity B-4.1 — Guiding Questions to Get Started

The guiding questions are designed to get you thinking and observing any actions the student or young adult has applied in learning or participating in events and other activities. The questions encourage you to drop all assumptions and keep an open mind. The fun and instructive part is noticing how the questions can provide understanding or help recall information that might lead to a productive exploration.

This exploration process involves recalling past experiences and conducting current observations to arrive at clues to a student's gift and strengths. There is no optimal time for doing this. You may want to revisit this process many times. Notes can be taken and discussed with others (i.e., teachers or professionals) on new insights noticed at one time, but forgotten. These clues could easily lead to new developing areas.

Note: In the following we refer to the "adolescent/young adult," recognizing that this individual's relationship to the person helping to complete this journey may be that of student, client, son/daughter, etc.

Is there something that would get the adolescent/young adult excited about each new day? If so, what would that be?

_____

_____

_____

What can the adolescent/young adult do well?

_____

_____

_____

Or what could the adolescent/young adult do well if he or she had time to practice and learn?

_____

_____

_____

What is her interest? passion?

_____

_____

_____

If all fears and anxiety could be wiped away about the adolescent/young adult's future, what dream would she explore and would you help her explore?

_____

_____

_____

If the adolescent/young adult could only do one thing with his life, what would that be?

_____

_____

_____

Does the adolescent/young adult lose track of time when involved in an activity? If so, what is the activity?

_____

_____

_____

Does she love the challenge of figuring out a problem? If so, what?

_____

_____

_____

Is he curious about a specific thing? If so, what is it?

_____

_____

_____

When she has a choice between something to learn or being entertained, how often is the learning experience chosen? How often is the entertaining experience chosen?

_____

_____

_____

Does the adolescent/young adult pursue an interest beyond the time others might pursue?

_____

_____

_____

Does the adolescent/young adult delight in learning something specific?

_____

_____

_____

Activity B-4.2 — Tune into Messages That Reveal Gifts or Interests

List any insights you have noticed. For example, can you recall:

An idea to explore an interest that might come from a story or a movie that the adolescent watched with his friends, or his class?

_____

_____

_____

_____

A place mentioned that may reveal his interest?

_____

_____

_____

_____

A hobby or activity that someone else has done that attracts the adolescent/young adult's attention with a bit of energy?

_____

_____

_____

An idea or interest that makes one stop and think?

_____

_____

_____

The adolescent/young adult's reactions to what he saw or heard?

_____

_____

_____

An environment or setting that seemed to appeal to the adolescent/young adult?

_____

_____

_____

Associates/friends from the past or present who had characteristics or personalities that brought out the best in the adolescent/young adult?

_____

_____

_____

A time the adolescent/young adult was sad? Be open and aware of what the individual feels or thinks about, even the sad and lonely feelings. Many of us do not want to focus on these emotions, but if we don't know what makes a person sad, how will we know when she feels good about herself? Additionally, how will we know to guide her to areas that help her feel good about whom she is or who she can become?

_____

_____

_____

Activity B-4.3 — Read and Consider Ideas Discovered from the Following Categories

Below are areas where gifts, skills, or interests may be found. This is in no way a complete list. Read through the areas to start thinking about what the adolescent/young adult can do or may enjoy exploring.

Listening:
- Does the adolescent/young adult like listening to stories? If so, what kind?
- Does she show others how much she enjoys their company by giving them particular attention?
- Does the adolescent/young adult enjoy listening and participating within a group of people who are working toward a common goal (e.g., Sunday School class, environmental group, or planning committee for a fund-raising task)?

Showing someone how to do a task:
- Can the adolescent/young adult show someone how to do a task?
- Does the adolescent/young adult know how to prepare a meal?
- Can he assist someone, then later show the steps? If so, what is the task?
- Can she show another person how to do something, such as fix hair, put on make-up, arrange flowers, water and care for plants, put oil in a car, or wash a car?

Reading:
- Can the adolescent/young adult read about what interests him?
- Is he interested in going to the library?
- Can he use the computer to look up his favorite topic on the Internet?
- Does he read and learn new words that can help him get around the neighborhood or run errands?

Writing:
- Does the adolescent/young adult make lists? If so, what kind?
- Can she take a phone message and write down a phone number?
- Does she have an email address?
- Can she read an email?
- If the words are too hard, can someone help her read email?
- Does she want to make a new friend and chat through email? (you may want to get help with this)

Computer:
- Does the adolescent/young adult know how to enter data into the computer?
  If not, is he interested in learning?
  If so, can an assistant, peer tutor, or parent help?

Painting/crafts:
- Does the adolescent/young adult like to paint, play with clay or wood, or sculpt?
- If she hasn't tried it, do you think she would like to take a class at a local art store or an adult class?
- Can an assistant or an art student who is a peer helper go with her?

Being still:
- Does the adolescent/young adult like to sit quietly and watch something of interest?
- Does he like to watch birds?
- Does he like to observe other animals, their behaviors, and responses?

Scientists make new discoveries by sitting quietly and watching behaviors. Scientists discover ways animals can help humans. Watching helps people appreciate how animals play, find food, care for their young can lead to ways to learn more. An assistant could explore this activity with a student by visiting the zoo and just sitting and watching the animals. This provides quiet downtime, which is calming and relaxing.

Approaching a task with willingness:
- Is the adolescent/young adult open to learn something new?
- Can she try a new skill or task and be evaluated only by her willingness? If so, recognize this is a mark of success.

At first, just let go of how well she does the task. Getting past the first step opens the door to learning how to do the task, one step at a time. So often demonstration of willingness is not recognized as a valid positive effort. Doing the task to completion is the goal, not the total success.

Organizing or categorizing items:
- Does the adolescent/young adult like to see items or objects in a certain order?
- Can he arrange things, such as his clothes in a closet, tools in the garage, or cartons of food in the refrigerator?
- If he enjoys this, explore ways to find a chore or a job organizing or arranging.

Sports:
- Does the adolescent/young adult enjoy a specific sport? If so, what kind?
- Can he find a team to join? If he cannot to play, could he volunteer?
- Could he be a spectator for his favorite team?

Exercise:
- Does the adolescent/young adult like to exercise?
- Is there a gym or YMCA she can join?
- What kind of exercise does she like or might she want to try?

Enjoying music:
- What music does the individual enjoy?
- Does he listen to it in his room at home with family?
- Does he go to a concert? Play an instrument?
- How can he share his favorite music with others? Is there a fan club to join?

Singing:
- Does the adolescent/young adult sing?
- Does she have a favorite singer?
- What kind of music does the singer sing?
- Can an assistant find a choir or a choral group for the individual to join?

Dancing:
- Does the adolescent/young adult like to dance?
  If she does not know, introduce dance to the student through a peer art/dance student.
- If she likes dance, what kind of dancing?
- Can the assistant find a club or a class where she could explore dance?
  That is, dancing with others, meeting new people?

Participating in an audience:
- Does the adolescent/young adult like to watch others sing and dance?
- Can the assistant find festivals or community events where she can go and enjoy the entertainment?

Remember, entertainers need an audience in order to express their gifts. The person sitting in the audience and appreciating the performance becomes a gift to the entertainer.

Activity B-4.4 — Make a Commitment

Provided in this activity are ideas the advocate may use with the adolescent/young adult in teaching the concept of making a commitment. It may be too overwhelming for the individual to focus on more than one idea at a time. If healthy food choices are an area of concern or need, guide the student to make a commitment to eat more of the healthy foods. Arrange for the adolescent/young adult to create a display with pictures of foods that show healthy meals. Offer him materials to cut out pictures and then paste them on a poster board. The fun part would include tasting the healthy foods. Prepare a visual and encourage the adolescent/young adult to check off all the healthy foods he or she has eaten each day. Record positive choices made in other areas and with other people. Point out any successful choices the student has made in his commitment.

Activity B-4.5 — Gifts and Talents Action Plan (GTAP)

When applying this activity to help someone who needs more support, the assistant will be the one to write a Gifts and Talents Action Plan. See the example below.

1. My goal for guiding my student or child to discover strengths is

    _____

2. I will have achieved this by_____(date)

3. I know I will have achieved it because I will

    _____

    and feel_____

    _____

    or be able to_____

    _____

Here is an example of how the GTAP works.

1. My goal in guiding a student/my adolescent to discover her gifts: <u>I will arrange for her to participate in two new activities.</u>

2. I will have helped her achieve participation in these two activities within the <u>Next month.</u>

3. I know I will have achieved it because <u>I will actively list the insights/clues in those activities that may spark her interest.</u>

    <u>We feel good about taking an action step toward guiding my adolescent/young adult.</u>

The goal below is an example of how **not** to approach exploring a gift. It is too huge and vague.

1. My goal is to <u>Find a gift or interest in the adolescent/young adult.</u>

2. I will have achieved this by <u>The end of the school year.</u>

3. I know I will have achieved it because <u>The adolescent/young adult will enjoy participating in the activity, start making friends, and have less behavioral issues.</u>

    And feel <u>Successful and accomplished.</u>

Activity B-4.6 — Imagine Your Future

The purpose here is to explore *how* the adolescent/young adult chooses her life to be, not *what* she wants to do. Often teachers or counselors ask students to think about a career or job when high school ends. Choosing a career is important, but other factors must be considered. In other words, imagining a job or career is not the purpose of this task. This activity encourages an examination of those things that reflect the adolescent/young adult's preferences, learning styles, and comfort levels around different people and environments.

Think about the kind of life that the student/individual would thrive in and enjoy if given the opportunity. Envision her life as one that would also meet her learning style, personal needs, and strengths.

Visualize images that are enriching with no boundaries or limits. Just for now, mentally set aside the requirement that the student/young adult needs certain supports. If you are or could be his main voice, what would he hope you would advocate? How would he hope that you would represent him?

This exercise requires the person and her support team to imagine an ideal life. If the person is severely disabled, use cut-out pictures, and so on, to help her communicate about desires, where to live, people doing things she may want to do (employment or hobbies). Include people who know her well in the activity. If the support team or family members recognize that she enjoys a slow and easy day, reflect that in the responses. You may not have an answer for each task or question. That's okay; the exercise encourages the advocate to start thinking about the kind of life that the adolescent/young adult may enjoy and even flourish in if she had the opportunity.

Things the adolescent/young adult has.

_____

_____

_____

People in her life (e.g., friends, coworkers). This may be people the adolescent/young adult has not yet met.

_____

_____

_____

Where does she live? What do the surroundings look like? In the city busting with people or on a quiet street?

_____

_____

_____

_____

Is the adolescent/young adult working with his hands or using physical strength?

_____

_____

_____

_____

What kind of work is he doing? What skills is he using?

_____

_____

_____

_____

What kinds of products or services do you see the adolescent/young adult working around?

_____

_____

_____

_____

What level of responsibility does she have?

_____

_____

_____

_____

What is the rhythm of the adolescent/young adult's day? (examples: slow and easy, quick pace, relaxed)

_____

_____

_____

_____

What hobbies and other interests do you see the adolescent/young adult pursuing?

_____

_____

_____

_____

What kinds of help do you see the adolescent/young adult offering to others?

_____

_____

_____

_____

Activity B-4.7 — Just for Fun, Pretend

Brainstorm ways to initiate this activity with the adolescent/young adult by combining settings and trying new experiences.

For example, consider the activity of "dancing." Here are some ideas to try. The adolescent/young adult attends a ballet/play, community festival, or watches a music/dance video. Involve a peer helper/student who knows "dance" to teach movement to various kinds of music. The feeling nature of music and dance cuts across all groups of people and language barriers. It can be fun and uplifting. A form of imagining involves senses of touch, music, and movement as in dance.

Integrate the activity with a literature-based reading assignment or a social studies unit. Learning about what other people, famous or everyday heroes, have accomplished or have become is the key here. For adolescents/young adults who have more severe disabilities, read or invite a student or a guest to read a story about people who are famous because they once contributed something valuable to the world.

You might try showing a video about what others have done in their lives or careers. Then ask the adolescent/young adult to draw a picture, write a story, or dress up and act out a skit revealing that particular career. To go one step beyond, take the adolescent/young adult into the community to observe, assist, or interview a person associated with that career or hobby.

The purpose is to guide the adolescent/young adult by offering information through various venues to help him understand that everyone has value, including the adolescent/young adult you are guiding. There are many ways to pursue this activity by brainstorming creative ideas and collaborating with others for support to pursue the activity with the individual. The assistance can come from anyone: peer students, university students, or volunteers from the community.

Activity B-4.8 — Create a Collage

This activity encourages the adolescent/young adult to start dreaming and choose or imagine his own life today and in the future. Gather brochures, advertisements, and photos, then offer the adolescent/young adult the opportunity to cut out and paste them on a large poster board. Making a collage of all things he would like to have may offer a sense of control and desire in his life.

Do not discourage choices of expensive and unaffordable options. Don't be concerned that you are leading the adolescent/young adult to false hopes.

If the adolescent/young adult chooses to buy a new car, don't stop there. Examine why a particular car was her choice. If the adolescent/young adult can verbalize, ask these questions:
- What is it about the car she likes?
- Is it the color, the size, or where the car will take her?
- Ask her where she would drive the car if she had one. Who would be in the car with her?
- What places and activities would she choose to try if she had the new car?

There is much to learn about a person's choices. All we have to do is observe and listen to see where it will take us.

False Hopes

Let's address the issue of false hopes. It may be true that the student will never be able to drive. Yet it is the natural feeling of possibilities that is the purpose of this exercise, and if it sparks hope and positive energy toward establishing control over one's life and building self-worth, the exercise is doing its job.

Activity B-4.9 — What Is Positive and Useful About Skills and Gifts?

This exercise requires the advocate to look closely at skills and gifts. List all the benefits an activity may provide the adolescent/young adult that may get him excited. This could provide insight into a particular job or hobby that will increase meaning and participation in the person's life.

List all the positive and useful things about some of these skills and gifts. For example, caring for a pet involves taking the dog for a walk, playing ball, feeding, bathing, petting, and teaching the dog tricks. Some of these tasks in combination could be a service that could be offered to neighbors or friends.

Some examples will get you thinking about where to search a person's skills and interests. Go ahead and list all the useful tasks in each of these areas.

- Enjoying activities out-of-doors _____

  _____

- Cooking or baking _____

  _____

- Shopping at the grocery store _____

  _____

- Church activities _____

  _____

- Gardening _____

  _____

- Riding a bike _____

  _____

- Computer games _____

  _____

- An unusual thing you can do that no few can do (for example, whistle) _____

  _____

- Taking something apart _____

  _____

- Arranging parts of something into a whole _____

  _____

We often ask adolescents/young adults to think in terms of a place or a career they may want some day. Although that has value, for those who need more support, try examining isolated skills and gifts apart from careers and occupations. Otherwise, certain valuable characteristics and tasks may go unnoticed because of an overemphasis on "occupations" or increasing "independent skills" become visible.

Activity B-4.10 — Your Skills

Guide the adolescent/young adult to recognize the skills he has. Include skills that are not just academic, any apparent skill that has a purpose and value. Talk with family members about the skills they notice at home. Some examples of skills and gifts I have noticed in my son include painting, organizing shelf items, serving as a cooking assistant, greeting visitors at an art fair, packaging items, assisting, and doing yard work.

List below the skills the adolescent/young adult has. Rate them by how much she enjoys them. Circle the top four or five. (Remember, a skill is something one has learned to do. Skills can be gifts, too. An interest is something that draws one's attention.)

Below list the skills in the numbered column and rate your skills based on the person's most favorite (10) and your least favorite (1).

List Skills	Rate Skills from 10-1
1. _____	_____
2. _____	_____
3. _____	_____
4. _____	_____
5. _____	_____
11. _____	_____
12. _____	_____
13. _____	_____
14. _____	_____
15. _____	_____
16. _____	_____

Activity B-4.11 — What Is One of Your Interests or Gifts?

This activity can include interests or gifts. Just a reminder: *An interest is something that draws attention; a gift is something one is born with, and a gift is something one does almost as easy as breathing.*

Take one of the interests from the activity. Using the process below, choose an interest and brainstorm ways it may be used. Then choose three more interests and brainstorm ways to use them. Read the two examples below.

Bobby has an interest in trains. What could he do with this interest?
- Building train stations is fun.
- There are people who have the same hobby.
- Bobby can talk to others who are interested in the same hobby. He can hang out at the local hobby store around others who like trains.
- He can read hobby magazines and find events on having this hobby.
- He can show someone how to build parts of a train village.
- Bobby can write about his hobby through email or on Internet sites.
- He can find a paid job in a hobby store assembling train stations and villages.

Carol has an interest in painting. What could she do with this interest?
- Painting is fun.
- She could use a paint brush to mix different colors of paint. Discovering new colors is nurturing and calming.
- Using her paint brush to make different lines and using various mediums and textures are interesting to her.
- It is fun to create interesting shapes and surfaces.
- She can collaborate with other artists in art projects.
- Painting around other people who are artists helps Carol make new friends. Her talent is appreciated by other artists as well.
- She shares her art with others.
- She can sell her paintings.
- She can shake hands and meet new people at art fairs and disability conferences where her work is exhibited. She is learning how her art is a contribution that people enjoy and value. She receives positive feedback when people comment that her paintings are beautiful.

Get out a clean sheet of paper. After reading the above, choose an interest the adolescent/young adult has, then brainstorm ways to use it. See how many different lists of interests you can write down and ways to explore them.

Activity B-4.12 — Gifts, Interests, and Environment Sheet

This activity seeks to list the adolescent/young's (a) gifts/skills or strengths, (b) interests, and (c) environments she may already enjoy and/or places she seeks to experience. Use information from activities already completed. The pictorial of clouds represents the highest thinking about the adolescent/young skills, gifts, and interests. An example is provided.

Activity B-4.12 Gifts, Interests, and Environment Sheet (Example)

Gifts/skills or strengths I have

- Painting on my canvas
- Being a part of, being included in family activities, games, outings
- Listening to jazz, blues, classical music
- Helping my grandmother with some yard work; I like clipping bushes best
- Cooking and baking

Interests — things I enjoy or want to try

- Expressing myself more fully.
- Shopping at the mall for NIKE shirts
- Horseback riding
- Travel
- Going to more sporting events
- Own my house
- Friends of my own

Environments (places) I enjoy or want to experience more often

- Being part of a church
- Going on a vacation with my family
- Eating in a nice restaurant
- Being in pleasant settings where pop music is played
- Colorful items and environments
- Places where I have several choices
- Places where people are willing to help and understand my needs

Activity B-4.12 My Gifts, Interests, and Environment Worksheet

Gifts/skills or strengths I have

Interests — things I enjoy or want to try

Environments (places) I enjoy or want to experience more often

Activity B-4.13 — Look at Your Possibilities

Brainstorm possible ways in which the adolescent/young adult can use his skills, gifts, and interests in various environments. Find the adolescent/young adult's gifts and skills listed in the top-left cloud on the Gifts, Interests, and Environment Sheet, Activity B-4.12. Next, using the Dream Sheet on page 167, write one skill or gift in each of the five cloud headings.

Think about each skill and interest and brainstorm a list of places where it can be practiced or offered to an organization, club, or community setting. Several options may emerge that can help the adolescent/young adult meet new people, have a hobby, volunteer, or even develop a job. The ideas may be helpful in educational planning.

Activity B-4.13 — Dream Sheet (Example)

Painting

- Take art lessons at adult learning centers or art stores.
- Create with other artists in a studio.
- Paint and donate my art to clubs, churches.
- Sell my art at community festivals and events.
- Exhibit my art in local coffee shops.

Being a part of: spending time with my family and participating with others in a group

- Listen to rock and blues bands.
- Get a job and assist a coworker at a job in the lawn dept.
- Watch a ballgame and participate in the chants.
- Visit art museums and collect books of famous artists and their paintings.
- Display my art at a disability conference.

Music: jazz, blues, classical

- Listen to the church choir.
- Sing in the church choir.
- Invite artist friends to cook out and play loud music.
- Attend community music festivals.

Outside: walking and yard work

- Walk my dog in the park daily.
- Paint a rug outside and give it to my grandma.
- Help my grandmother clip her bushes.
- Participate in an outside art festival selling my work.

Cooking and baking

- Paint the fruits and vegetables I like to cook and eat.
- Get a job in a coffee shop where art is displayed.
- Prepare a dinner with help and invite my family to an outside picnic.

Activity B-4.13 — My Dream Sheet

Activity B-4.14 — Look for Your Themes

As an advocate for the adolescent/young adult, collaborate with the individual him/herself, family members, and others in responding to the following questions. The answers involve an assessment of what matters to the adolescent/young adult and can lead him or her to areas of interests that could lead to a higher quality of life. Brainstorm ideas that may become beneficial and determine possible actions to take toward guiding the student or young adult to realize opportunities of participation. The new information could lead to areas and activities to pursue that can launch him forward to a higher level of participation and active involvement.

Does the adolescent/young adult like to work with his hands, use tools, plants, the earth, or other materials?

_____

_____

_____

_____

Do he prefer to participate by himself, with another person, or in a group of people?

_____

_____

_____

_____

Did your list show that the adolescent/young adult prefers a physical activity? If so, was he moving around in one environment by himself or with other people?

_____

_____

_____

_____

How does this activity benefit others or provide a service to help someone else?

_____

_____

_____

Does the list show that the adolescent/young adult enjoys being around people with whom she has a common interest? If so, what are those interests?

_____

_____

_____

_____

_____

Does the adolescent/young adult have an interest that could lead to learning a new skill? For example, if his interest is related to pets, what new training or skills could be taught?

_____

_____

Is that new skill useful or fun? Is it a service?

_____

_____

Can the new skill be used in daily living?

_____

_____

Could the skill or gift eventually be a way to earn an income?

_____

_____

Is the skill or gift useful all year round or only at certain times of the year; for example, holidays?

_____

_____

Is the skill or gift useful for a particular season only (e.g., summer)?

_____

_____

_____

_____

What themes were prevalent on the list?

_____

_____

_____

_____

Activity B-4.15 — You Say, "I Can't"

This activity is useful for adolescents/young adults who may be considered low functioning. Set this up as a game and start with tasks you know she can do. For instance, do you remember a time when she rejected doing a task? Tell the adolescent/young adult, "I have seen you do this task. You are telling me with your actions that you can."

At times adolescents/young adults become overdependent on a parent, team member, or teacher. For example, suppose you are aware that the adolescent/young adult can pour his own milk into his cereal, but is waiting for help. Catch him doing certain tasks successfully and say, "You just did it." To confront resistance, make a chart with words or pictures of all the tasks the adolescent/young adult can do. Take photos or video tape of him participating in these tasks. Emphasize "YOU CAN!"

Activity B-4.16 — Now Say, "I Can"

Arrange for the student to make a large collage of all the things she can do. It may include brushing teeth or feeding a pet. It may be giving a hug, smiling or laughing at an older brother acting goofy. Simply emphasize the CAN DO belief.

Activity B-4.17 — Building Your Self-Worth

Make a list with the adolescent/young adult of all the positive traits you have noticed. The list can include a skill, gift, or an attribute. Don't only use academic skills. For example, note items from having pretty eyes, using the Internet well, to lifting and moving heavy furniture and boxes. The idea is to build self-worth, no matter what it is based upon.

Activity B-4.18 — More on Building Your Self-Worth

A situation may arise where the adolescent/young adult is confronting another person's doubt about her ability in some area. Encourage her to express what is bothering her about what the other person is saying. Help her see ways of becoming capable in these areas.

Offer this activity to a student who is encountering someone who is rude or intolerable. Ask the student to draw a picture of the person who said the negative comment as a goofy, silly figure. Next, ask the student to draw a big **X** through it. Another option is to write a letter to the person who is intolerable in the student's defense (don't really mail it). For example, the student writes a letter (with the parent or teacher's help) to the next-door neighbor. Dear Joe, "You are a jerk; I really can cut the grass." This activity helps the student make a step toward recognizing comments by others that are rude. It also guides the student to be proactive in valuing his or her own needs. Lastly, it takes the focus off others' rudeness and the student's negative attitude toward the individual.

If the other person's rudeness toward the adolescent/young adult is severe, this activity may only be a start. Other forms of proactive supports may be necessary.

Activity B-4.19 — What If Failure Isn't Possible?

This activity can be helpful for individuals with severe disabilities or significant behavioral issues. Brainstorm an interest that the adolescent/young adult chooses to pursue in the home, school, or community setting. Select a fun activity that the adolescent/young adult has never tried. Try to eliminate any interferences that could prevent success. Allow for peers or classmates to assist for support. Take pictures during the outing. When the adolescent/young adult engages in the event with success, use the pictures as a mark of accomplishment and overcoming failure. If the event results in difficulty for any reason, emphasize that no attempt is ever a failure. New information can be learned from any experience.

Ask the following questions:

• What can be learned from the experience?

_____

_____

_____

• What supports can be offered so improved success will become the result?

_____

_____

_____

• What part of the experience will be set aside and later initiated as the adolescent/young adult becomes more comfortable?

_____

_____

_____

• For example, if the adolescent/young adult was not able to endure the entire event, will decreasing the amount of time involved in the activity promote success?

_____

_____

_____

Activity B-4.20 — Test Your Motivation

The adolescent/young adult may lack motivation to do a task or learn something new because she fears failure, has sensory issues, or does not see a purpose to the activity. Assist her in choosing a task that you think she will find enjoyable if given the opportunity.

Ideas may be as basic as baking cookies, preparing a simple meal, taking a walk in a new park, writing a poem or a story, drawing a picture, or learning to ride a bicycle. As you complete the activity, do the following:

• Write down the adolescent/young adult's willingness throughout the process.

• Take pictures of the adolescent/young adult's receptiveness so the student will recognize success.

• Place the success pictures in a personal book or frame them for viewing.

• Discuss the event and the success before going out again for continued growth in addressing willingness to try, a subpart of motivation.

• Commit to initiating activities until the adolescent/young adult has developed more acceptance and benefits from the experience. Keep trying until progress is achieved. It may require many attempts to achieve a degree of success.

This activity can build the adolescent/young adult's motivation, capability levels, and self-determination.

Activity B-4.21 — Revisit, Imagine Your Future

Guide the adolescent/young adult who has discovered a new dream. Help him express his dream(s), what he wants to become. Don't judge his dream as being silly or outlandish. Just offer him a way to express himself by writing a story, through art media, a song, and so on.

Activity B-4.22 — How Setting a Goal Can Help

Preparing for the future is difficult. Review and ponder the following questions about goal setting to increase quality of life. It is important to explore these questions although you may not know the answers. They provide a direction that may need to be taken. It will help to draw team support for discussing these questions that can lead to setting goals.

- What needs to happen in the adolescent/young adult's life this week, this month, this year, for the next five years?

_____

_____

_____

- What problems need to be solved? (examples: adapting to community settings, getting a driver's license, finding a job, engaging in a hobby)

_____

_____

_____

- What material things does he need or want to have? (e.g., a guitar, car, computer, an apartment)

_____

_____

_____

- What work or activities would be beneficial to further his development?

_____

_____

_____

Activity B-4.23 — Turn All Your Desires and Dreams into a Goal

Below are some important ideas that can help you, the assistant, maintain goals. I found these ideas helpful (Beattie, 1987, pp. 157-158).

A solution to a problem may be found by setting a goal. When the adolescent/young adult has an unmet need, make achieving it a goal. If the adolescent/young adult has a significant disability and has become isolated in the home, the goal may be getting out and participating more in the community. Seek help in finding support. Review the adolescent/young adult's interests and strive for success regardless of where he is functioning.

What is it the adolescent/young adult needs to function more successfully? Turn it into a goal, whether it is camping or shopping at the mall. When the adolescent/young adult has a problem, make solving it a goal. What will bring her joy, relief, or opportunity for growth? Is it a new black leather jacket, or a membership at the YMCA to work out? Turn it into a goal. Does the adolescent/young adult enjoy a leisure activity, such as camping, shopping at the mall, attending a concert starring her favorite entertainer? Does she want friendships, a club or place to belong to?

Turn making a decision into a goal. Does she want to start painting?

Think big about finding solutions to problems.

Power comes to those who write down goals rather than just loosely storing them in their minds. By writing down goals with the adolescent/young adult, you create focus and organization. I discovered that, once I put my goals and dreams on paper, I released the outcome. Hang the goals in a place where they can be seen, such as the refrigerator, bulletin board, or the bathroom mirror.

Encourage the adolescent/young adult to mark his progress in working on goals. This gives him confidence to keep at it. Teach him to congratulate himself and celebrate as the goal is reached. Point out that good things do happen.

Be patient. Trust that your goal will be solved given the right timing. Don't ever say, "Oh, this problem will never go away. Or this dream will never come true."

A goal I want to work on:

_____

_____

_____

_____

Activity B-4.24 — Recognizing People Who Support You

There are many social issues surrounding adolescents/young adults with a disability. Unfortunately, they often encounter bullies and are subjected to ridicule. It is confusing to understand how to respond to a bully or someone who rude.

It is important that the adolescent/young adult knows who is a support. This exercise can help facilitate an understanding of the peers who are supportive versus those who are not. Guide the adolescent/young adult in choosing names and pictures of people who are helpful and kind. Discuss what traits these helpful individuals have.

Always keep an open dialogue with the adolescent/young adult and investigate any situation where others are disrespectful. Develop supports to help the student understand whom to trust.

Inside the circle on page 181, write down the names of people the adolescent/young trusts (parents, teachers, classmates, peer tutors, employer, coworkers, etc.). Also put down names of people who are supportive of the adolescent/young adult's interests (parents, friend, aunt, a teacher, etc.). The names placed in the inside circle are the people with whom the adolescent/young adult knows he is safe. Outside the circle, place names of people who may not be the adolescent/young adult's best allies or represent his best interests. For example, put Sally's name on the outside of the circle because she is a girl who laughs and teases.

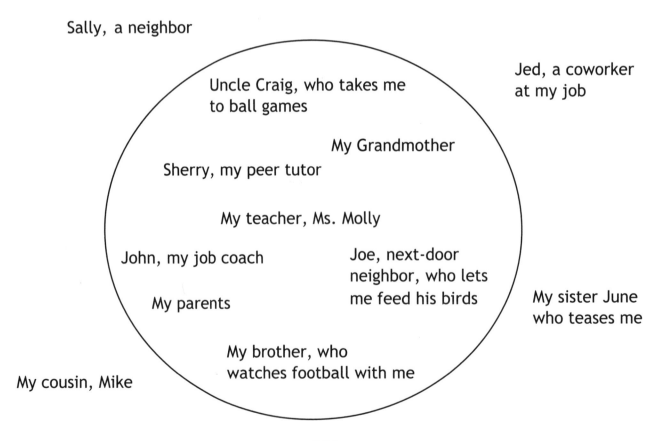

Sally, a neighbor

Jed, a coworker at my job

Uncle Craig, who takes me to ball games

My Grandmother

Sherry, my peer tutor

My teacher, Ms. Molly

John, my job coach

Joe, next-door neighbor, who lets me feed his birds

My parents

My sister June who teases me

My brother, who watches football with me

My cousin, Mike

Now it is your turn.

Activity B-4.25 — Finding Time

This activity focuses on the person who is guiding the adolescent/young adult. Because so much of the support is due to the person who is guiding the adolescent/young adult through the process, it is important to take a look at the time you are spending. In this case, we are using the example of a parent. Doing daily errands, therapy, school, and so on, takes up time. As the adolescent/young adult's family/advocate you may say that you don't have time to explore your daughter's gifts and interests.

It helps to look closer at how you are spending your time. Where does your time go? List activities your daughter did this past week. You might notice time to spare for a new activity, or you might schedule the necessary downtime or alone time just for you and your daughter.

Activity B-4.26 — What Activities Do You Enjoy?

This activity is intended to draw support from people who know the adolescent/young adult, such as a family member, a peer, or team member. The task may involve recalling an experience or event that was once useful and positive for the adolescent/young adult and doing it again.

The questions become:

- What were the activities she once enjoyed?

- How can she participate in them again?

- How often does she get the opportunity to enjoy the activity?

Things She Enjoys Doing	Date She Last Did the Activity	Check the Activities That Might Be Tried Again
_____	_____	_____
_____	_____	_____
_____	_____	_____
_____	_____	_____
_____	_____	_____
_____	_____	_____
_____	_____	_____
_____	_____	_____
_____	_____	_____
_____	_____	_____
_____	_____	_____
_____	_____	_____

Activity B-4.27 — "Living Your Life" Pie and Giving Back to Yourself

Adolescents/young adults with more severe disabilities need to know that they have the right to access options that release stress and are enjoyable. Sometimes we are so focused on working toward correcting a person's behavior that we neglect to think of ways that she can reduce stress.

With the demands of school, therapy, and so on, the adolescent/young adult may not have many chances to learn how to react, enjoy, or appreciate less stressful times. In addition, she may not be able to verbalize what is enjoyable or desired. These reactions must be taught, pointed out, and explained to the adolescent/young adult, because she has a basic right to experience "relaxed, stress-free, enjoyable times." We can help by naming it when teaching a strategy that is calming and relaxing.

Some examples include
- listening to soothing music
- deep breathing
- exercising or
- just having quiet time

There are many alternatives to explore and find those that work for the adolescent/young adult.

Activity B-4.28 — Choose a Role Model

Observe what the adolescent/young adult's interests are. If Jimmy's interest is basketball, does he admire certain players? A team? A coach? If his interest is a musical group, who does he enjoy and why? If he does not name or have a role model, expose Jimmy to information/situations involving his interest that may reveal a role model. Once known, help the adolescent/young adult contact the role model through a letter, email, or even get to meet the role model in person, if possible. Don't forget to take a picture.

Susan

Introducing Susan: Susan has enjoyed music since she was a small child and has many role models who are singers in the entertainment field.

Susan says, "Life without music is unimaginable. If a life is a life without music, it's boring," Susan said. "I don't care what kind of music it is — I love it."

Susan takes music classes at the community college and lives in an apartment with a roommate. She has appeared on several national talk shows. Her mother said, "Susan is a compassionate young woman who wants to teach others about what it is like to live with a disability, Williams Syndrome."

Activity B-4.29 — The *Remarkably Able* College-Bound Student

Students with severe disabilities are now increasingly entering college. As a high school teacher or parent who is guiding the adolescent/young adult to prepare for college, you will find this activity helpful. Initiate a project to explore all the tasks necessary for preparing for college. This may be a semester project involving the student in preparing and planning for this major transition stage. Class credit could be offered if the student writes or reports what she learned. The project may also be carried out at home or in other settings.

Persons with disabilities may require additional support to successfully attend college. Those supports can range from a technical device, to a learning strategy, or taking tests without a time limit.

Independent living skills are usually taught in high school and encouraged as the young adult goes to college. Unfortunately, that is usually not enough. When striving to function at higher levels such as college, the adolescent/young adult must also learn to let go or give up some preferred activities or comfortable habits:

- Decrease the length of time involved in preferred activities (e.g., computer time)
- Give up sleeping late into the morning
- Give up a familiar routine and recreate a new schedule

The question becomes, What will the individual give up in order to make room for a new venture such as college? We must help the adolescent/young adult recognize that he may have to let go of some of the time usually spent doing preferred activities. It is not suggested that the adolescent/young adult stop doing these preferred activities, but the amount of time spent on them may need to be reduced. Enjoyable activities are important for relaxation between going to class and studying.

Here is a basic how-to process. It is not an unfamiliar process. Everyone has to go through this. Wanting to go to college and accomplishing it are two different things.

Jim

Jim wants to earn a degree in computer graphics. His goal is to work in the home office of a large pizza company in his home town.

How can he move from his current position at a small sign shop to acquiring a career with a large company?

How can he reach his dream profession and yet start within his world as it is?
- He will trade in his full-time job for a part-time job in order to take college courses.
- He will abandon his days of sleeping late and hours watching TV in order to allow time for taking classes.
- He will budget his cash in order to pay for updated computer software that will be used to increase his expertise and skill in designing graphics. This may leave him without spare cash for movies.
- He will trade his nights out with friends for hours of study to prepare for class assignments.
- He will trade his defensive ego for resilience and courage when he faces customers who want to order a sign. Many of these customers are very direct and unwilling to hear what a professional might recommend.

State a goal and list what the individual needs take the necessary steps toward the college goal.

_____

_____

_____

_____

_____

Assist the adolescent/young adult in examining her own qualities and list the ones that need improvement to enable her to attend college.

_____

_____

_____

_____

_____

_____

_____

List steps in the process.

_____

_____

_____

_____

_____

Review this list frequently to determine progress. Keep working at it and gradually address all qualities that need attention.

Below are important qualities that lead to success in college

Positive attitude — Try to look at the best in a situation. If you get a low grade on a test, ask yourself what you can learn from it. Maybe you can have a tutor before the next test. Is it possible you did not study long enough or misunderstood the major sections in your notes you were supposed to study?

Commitment — Be willing to go to class and study every day. Are you late for classes or often get lost? What can help you: a loud alarm clock or written directions to your destination?

Daily Satisfaction — Everyone gets frustrated. You may need to examine more closely the source of your frustration. If you are slipping behind academically, not getting to class on time, or not turning in important paperwork to the financial aid office, it may be a problem of organization. Don't blame others. Determine how you can organize these details better. Make a "to do" list for each task. Remember, do not hesitate to ask for help when you need it.

Balance — Be careful to schedule your day with a variety of activities. Are you getting enough sleep, physical exercise, and eating at least one good meal a day?

Feedback — This is tricky for many people. You may find out you misunderstood an assignment. Be willing to talk with your instructor or a fellow student and start your project all over again just to get it right.

Independence — Being independent does not mean you cannot ask for help or rely on advice from others. Expect as much independence from yourself as possible, but ask for assistance when in doubt. When you use problem-solving strategies to handle a situation, you are experiencing true growth and maturity. Just recognizing your effort is reinforcing. It keeps you focused and shows maturity and growth.

Understanding — Do you understand your academic strengths and challenges? Can you convey that to yourself, to another?

Flexibility — Be willing to assess your strengths and weaknesses and modify your goals, if necessary. If you like the health care field but cannot make the grades to become a nurse, perhaps you can become a nurse's aide. Millions of nondisabled persons have used this strategy to find a career. The same approach can work for individuals with a developmental disability. Who knows, the nurse's aide might become the nurse later on.

Recognize Strengths and Challenges

Consider these questions. The answers can help recognize the choices that can best promote success.

Is a small college campus with small class sizes appropriate? _____

_____

Are quiet environments best? _____

_____

Are explanations better understood when listening or when reading? _____

_____

Are models or diagrams helpful in understanding a difficult concept? _____

_____

Does the adolescent/young adult need assistance in moving to different settings? _____

_____

Does the adolescent/young adult understand an idea better when another person does it first, showing each step? _____

_____

Does the adolescent/young adult need extra time to read class assignments? _____

Take notes? Study for tests? _____

Does the adolescent/young adult benefit from frequent breaks during study time in order to stay focused on the material?_____

_____

If still in high school, what actions have been initiated to:

• take the ACT, SAT, or other entry tests? _____

• arrange a time to register for a tour at the school you are considering attending? _____

• write a list of questions to ask a counselor at the college? _____

Some of the areas to ask about when visiting a college include:

- tuition _____

- student grants and loans _____

- foreign language requirements _____

- number of credits required to complete an academic program _____

- campus dorms or apartment information _____

- clubs to join and activities that are interesting _____

- disability departments and the information they provide to students _____

Having an assistant might be required to get to classes, prepare and/or study for classes, join clubs, develop friendships, etc. Brainstorm options or seek help in this area.

- Procedures and rules for receiving assistance through the disability department. What are the deadlines for applications? _____

- Accommodations for test taking. Find out what steps to take and/or documentation to provide. _____

- Requirements such as letters of recommendation or entrance exams to submit to the advising counselor. _____

Develop Friendships at College

Associations and friendships can be developed by participating in some of these areas. Explore options:

- Part-time work study

- Study groups with other students

- Campuswide events where students and professors participate or meet

- Tutors or mentors

Activity B-4.30 — Personal Growth Outcomes

Other young adults have made positive changes in their lives. Their outcomes are noted below. If you have completed some of the activities in this section, you are on y our way to discovering possible ways to use your talents and strengths. An increased quality of life is sure to follow if you keep working on identifying and using y our strengths and gifts.

R   **raised group consciousness** through self-expression and contribution

E   exhibited **emotional** growth

M   **matured** through confronting challenges

A   knows and enjoys **acceptance** among others

R   takes **responsibility** for him/herself and others

K   gained **knowledge** of his/her limitations and capabilities

A   **appreciates** his/her place in life

B   participates as an owner in his/her **business**

L   **lives** in and is purchasing a home

Y   became a compassionate **young** adult teaching others through personal expression (i.e., singing, performing, and/or offering insights) so others can know how to support and respect people who have ASD and other disabilities

A   **appeared** and performed in entertainment venues, media, weddings, art exhibitions

B   created and painted **beautiful** pieces of art that allowed the artist to compete with other well known artists and win honors

L   enjoys **living** his or her own life

E   **employed** in a work that matches his or her skills and gifts

My research study involved in-depth interviews with parents about how the young adult with ASD was capable of full community living. One significant impact that brought success to each young adult included developing his or her self-expression by applying a gift, a strength, or a strong interest to an area that offered employment, leisure, or a connection to the community and to others.

Some of the young adults' gifts include:
- painting with acrylics
- playing classical music on the piano
- memorizing and analyzing various sports statistics
- excelling at bookkeeping
- strong interest in animated technology
- teaching parents and people with ASD how to use facilitated communication tools
- strong geographical knowledge and application
- caregiver — nurturing toward elderly and small children

Activity B-4.31 — Creating a MAP: MY ACTION PLAN

Steps in the Process

Now that you and the adolescent/young adult have spent a great deal of effort toward exploring gifts, strengths, talents, and interests, it is time to develop a personal MAP (My Action Plan). Have handy the answers to the activities you already completed. It is most helpful to complete this activity with a team that includes family members, professionals, neighbors, friends, and people who know the young adult in the community. The following steps are viewed from the parents' perspective.

1. Start with writing that highest vision the family and the adolescent/young adult have. A vision is a clear image of the future that can be attainable. You must have a vision that leads you in a specific direction.

2. Select one or more of the beliefs you listed in Beliefs and Principles about Independence. The belief (s) should reflect your concept of the highest attainable quality of life you have for your son or daughter.

3. Choose principles from Beliefs and Principles about Independence or write new ones. Make sure the principle(s) you selected is supported by one or more of your beliefs. Without that provision you cannot live by your principles. You can review the activities, especially Activity 4.6 to determine how you and the young adult view living his or her life.

4. Decide on particular goals to reach for your son or daughter. There may be several, but should have at least two. Some areas from Activity: 4.27 — Living your Life Pie include exercise, play, work, school, friends/companions, family activities and spirituality/church.

5. Determine activities necessary to achieve the goals you set. You may need to break each one into smaller and smaller activities until you can complete each within a week, or even a day.

6. The final step is to design an ideal weekly activity schedule. Update this list often and have it in view so you can look at it daily until you and your young adult have reached the goal(s).

For the first six months review and readjust the activities monthly. This process is about moving forward until the goal is reached.

The Vision

for Jennifer (an example)

Jennifer has autism, is nonverbal, yet lives a life uniquely her own. She has the supports to live in a house with two other roommates within an older, quiet neighborhood. She is active in the community, shopping, skating, and enjoying short vacations with peers her age. Jennifer is employed and earns an income by delivering mail and packages within a large governmental office complex. She pays her basic expenses and purchases clothes and other personal items with her income.

We (her parents) believe

Jennifer has the right to live her life with as much involvement and independence in the community as possible, even with her severe autism.

Jennifer's Gifts

She is a beautiful woman who shines brilliantly in her smiles and body language when she is doing what she enjoys (i.e., shopping, working on a task, and roller skating with others). She has a lot of energy and joy to offer when she has a structure and a schedule, and when others appreciate her efforts. She can follow through with all steps of a task, once she is taught. She categorizes well. Jennifer has shown these abilities with chores at home and in school library volunteer work.

Principle(s)

We will search for governmental supports and creative alternatives that will allow Jennifer to live fully in all aspects of the community.

Challenges

Jennifer has severe autism and will need 24-hour supervision. This will also include a job coach, agency support, and a community coach for outings.

Jennifer has had severe behavioral issues. She has worn a helmet at times to protect her head during episodes where she hit her head on the wall. However, with supports, she has not worn a helmet for nearly seven years.

Goal(s)

To find
- an agency that will provide services whereby Jennifer will reach the vision to live her life fully and independently with supports

- community coaches who will facilitate community leisure

- a job Jennifer will enjoy and can do with the support of a job coach or a coworker

Parental Activities

Options to consider that will help Jennifer live Independently:

- Inquire about Medicaid Waiver list; place Jennifer's name on the list.

- Interview representatives of agencies that provide services for individuals with disabilities to live in the community.

- Seek out two families who have a similar vision for their daughter and who may want to join with us to create options to establish a shared house and shared support.

- Seek HUD housing information for each woman to pay rent.

- Seek joint purchase of a house where Jennifer and the other women will pay subsidized rent to parents.

Options to consider for finding good community coaches:

- Seek a community coach to facilitate Jennifer's access to community settings. Network among friends, neighbors, church, and club associations for this support.

- Inquire about community coaches from college students who are interested in becoming therapists, teachers, nurses, etc., and who have great references.

- Seek respite or other funding to pay for Jennifer's care or community participation.

Employment

- Seek Vocational Rehabilitation eligibility. Access a counselor.

- Seek a provider agency that will offer help finding a job and a job coach to teach Jennifer the job.

- Seek information on self-employment. Many individuals with disabilities have started their own businesses to work with others and have support from others to do the tasks.

- Refer to results and insights from WP activities that revealed Jennifer's gifts, strengths, and interests and how those can be used to carve out a job.

MY ACTION PLAN
(MAP)

A vision is a clear image of the future that can be attainable.

The Vision

_____

_____

_____

_____

_____

Beliefs refer to why we live our life.

Our Beliefs

_____

_____

_____

Principles refer to how we live our life.

Our Principle(s)

_____

_____

_____

_____

Challenges

_____

_____

_____

_____

Goal One

_____

_____

_____

_____

Activities

_____

_____

_____

_____

_____

_____

_____

_____

Goal Two

_____

_____

_____

_____

Activities

_____

_____

_____

_____

_____

_____

_____

_____

_____

Goal Three

_____

_____

_____

_____

Activities

_____

_____

_____

_____

_____

_____

_____

_____

_____

Do not give up. Keep moving through this process. You never know when something will be revealed or appear, such as a new person who is willing to become a support to the individual, or an ideal work environment with the right supports in place to help the individual maintain his job.

CHAPTER FIVE:
WALKING THE PATH MODEL
Purposes and Advantages

The theme of this book is that people with disabilities, regardless of the severity, have strengths, gifts, and interests. Most important, their strengths, gifts, and interests can be easily identified and are useful in diverse areas of living and community settings. When an individual uses his or her best attributes, several benefits occur, including:

- increased meaning and purpose in daily activities

- greater positive feelings about what she is capable of doing, which can have an impact in reducing negative behaviors

- acceptance among the community, to include entry into employment and leisure settings

- personal growth over a period of time, which changes the individual's profile and capability levels (Greenspan & Wieder, 1998; Marquette, 2007)

None of this can happen without the collaboration across all role groups, the individual with a disability, family members, school personnel, professionals in the disability field, and policymakers.

The following chart illustrates the major topics addressed in this book and how they connect role groups to provide diverse types of supports for individuals with ASD and DD.

Positive External	Individual Outcomes	Self Determination & Personal Development	Supports (Gov., other created and negotiated)	Roles in Empowerment Process	Needs	Individuals with ASD DD Effects
Group Change: • School/or organizational programs. • Family: improved well-being & functioning • New policy development: positive organizational change/ supporting individuals with DD & ASD • Societal gains: contributing member or producer	**Health & well-being:** • Physical: nutritional healthy • Emotional development: positive or internal change; negative change • Self-acceptance & self-value increased • Increased capability/ independence in domains of living (even w/ supports)	**Quality in daily routine:** • Associates or friendships • Leisure/ exercise • Gift/strength identified, applying strengths to interests • Employment training or college • Communicating thoughts, & preferences Opportunity to practice self help skills Living independently with supports	**Government:** • SSI/SSDI, Medicaid waivers, supported living, healthcare People supports: • community coach, • live-in, • job coach, • coworker, • peer(s), • mentors Technical Assistance: • equipment, • organizational tools/strategies Community Supports (Society)/ Attitudes: positive, open, & willing to accept differences	**Individual w/ ASD or DD:** • Parent, guardian, or family advocate • Personnel in school or agency representative/or other • Collaboration Parent/ Guardian/ professional/ agency representatives • Councils: Education & Developmental Disability/ Other Policymakers	**Lack of:** • Education, income (job) • Transportation • Support & companionship • Community participation (living in isolation) • Choice and control over life • Opportunity to learn independent living skills healthy living, protection (exposure to violence)	Youth and Young Adults

What happens to people with disabilities when they grow up?

Steven Shore, a well-known advocate and person with autism, once commented that we rarely hear what happens to individuals with ASD after they turn 21. Research reveals *few* positive outcomes regarding young adults' post-high school years. Many become overdependent upon their families for daily living needs. Kantrowitz and Scelfo (*Newsweek*, November 27, 2006) reported that a new crisis is coming for youth with ASD as the families are asking, "What happens next?"

This crisis has been here for several decades; the numbers affected are just larger now. Indeed, the Centers for Disease Control have recently released the findings of a 2002 study that found rates of autism to be approximately 1 in 150 children (CDC Media Relations Press Release, 2007).

How can this situation be molded into producing more positive outcomes for youth? The solution is not simple, but doable. It involves multifaceted and multidimensional approaches. The WP model can launch youth into positive outcomes with practical steps on every level of involvement during transition. The WP model guides advocates and youth to:

- develop personal growth through positive self-awareness and self-expression within daily living

- uncover hidden gifts and talents

- network and create innovative options that will lead the individual to function at higher levels of capability

- create supports to use one's best strengths to facilitate transition and launch opportunities in community living; employment, self-employment, training, developing relationships, and independence

I had the privilege to hear Dr. Martin Seligman speak at a national school psychologists convention in 2005. I was inspired by his message. He spoke about how important it is to find what one is good at and to use our strengths to acquire meaning and positive engagement. Although he was not specifically speaking about persons with disabilities, I immediately saw the application of what he was advocating.

Seligman (2005b) stated, "We are here to find what we are good at." He later noted, "The traditional approach has been to find out what people are doing wrong, then to find ways to correct. We've been doing this, even though there is no data that supports the practice."

Seligman suggested that we ask, "What do we do right?" I suggest that that we translate that into asking, "What does Sally do right, or which skill or gift does she use well?" When a student's strength is recognized, we can guide her to use it in a larger capacity. Yet, how does exploring gifts work when a person has behavioral issues?

Advantage of Exploring and Using Gifts

*"Curing the negatives does not
produce the positives" (Seligman, 2006, p. iii).*

Let's view his quote in the context of people with disabilities and our work. Reshaping behavior is important to a person's overall functioning, but that in itself does not lead to quality of life. If we were able to help the person with ASD and DD reduce or get rid of all the adverse behaviors attributed to a disability, what is left? A person with no behavioral issues, which we would so cherish. Yet, what would the person have contributed?

There has to be an emphasis on finding and using strengths or gifts. We, the advocates, must direct positive energy toward providing the adolescent/young adult with experiences that highlight his or her strength and gifts. This, in turn, will promote personal growth, self-acceptance, and responsibility. So curing the negatives (behavioral issues) is not the solution. We must help youth produce the positives in life. When a person's strengths and gifts are highlighted, his or her weaknesses diminish.

The process of exploring strengths and gifts is for everyone, *especially* for those with moderate and severe behavioral or cognitive levels. Do not think in terms of the individual's functioning level, high, low, or in between. Throw these away as they have no use here. The WP is a process for all because gains can be made from any level.

The following diagrams illustrate the relationship between supports that manage behavior and supports that allow the individual to express his or her gift.

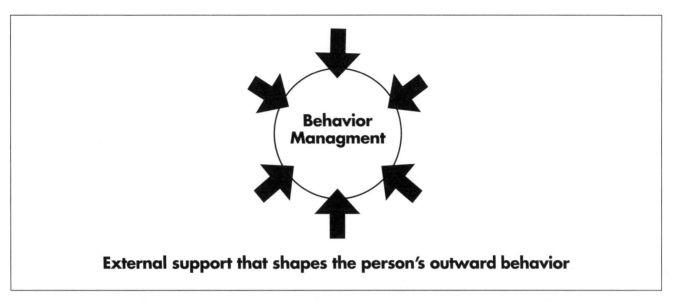

External support that shapes the person's outward behavior

External behavioral supports help an individual receive direction and internally control appropriate responses and behaviors. Supports are necessary for the adolescent/young adult to have opportunities to participate in a particular environment. These *supports* teach the person to self-regulate.

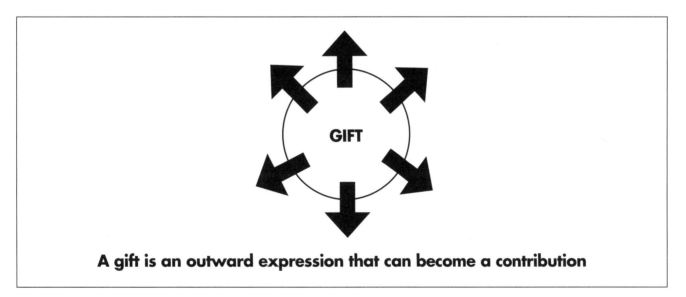

A gift is an outward expression that can become a contribution

A typical person's gift or strength is self-expressed, thus making a contribution. However, many individuals with ASD and DD are not able to offer a gift in this way because of a need for support to compensate for sensory issues or other limitations.

The following diagram shows that when supports are in place, the individual is highly capable of offering his gift or contribution.

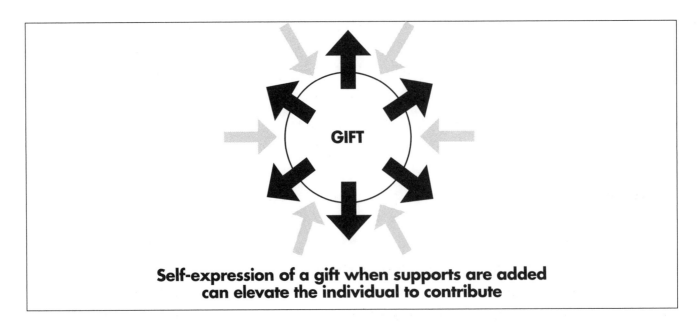

**Self-expression of a gift when supports are added
can elevate the individual to contribute**

Here the supports are the arrows pointing inward, lifting the individual to offer his gift or contribution. "Supports" are key. Offering the strength or gift builds self-awareness and self-acceptance, which in turn draws others to accept and respect the individual for his contribution.

How to Recognize a Strength or Gift

The following vignette describes how the process presented in Chapter Four can lead to a new employment opportunity. Let me introduce you to James, a young adult in his late 20s who has severe autism and is nonverbal. His strengths and gifts can be identified once we assume a more open attitude.

- We can explore where James fits in this world because something fascinating (an interest or a gift) can literally "touch" him, although we may not know what that something is.

- We can help James explore how to get in touch with that something that drives him (the gift). What makes his chimes ring and is his purpose in life.

- When the gift, interest, or strength emerges, we can help him develop and contribute, therefore, "touching" (contributing to) someone else.

- When James tries new things with our guidance, the process will enable him to get in touch with how he really feels. He may or may not be able to communicate in words, but he will tell us through his body language as he receives and gives. The delight in whole body movement, eyes, and smiles tells us what he is feeling. If he could verbalize what his body says, he would say, "I'm more in touch with myself" because I am working in a preschool preparing snacks for children. I love their laughter and the activity that children offer.

About James. James has an independent living arrangement and resides in a small apartment upstairs in his mother's house. The apartment was built for that purpose. His mother says that James is "low-functioning" with an IQ in the low 20s. She has been a strong advocate and was adamant that he have a high quality of life and participate in areas where he could make a contribution despite his disability. James is served by an agency that provides the support of an assistant, who introduces him to a variety of activities in the community. Such people supports also helped James get a part-time job at a preschool.

His mother claims that the autism diagnosis has no relevance to what James pursues in life. The people who surround James are his team of support. They have identified his strengths as follows:

1. staying focused with all the steps of a task (once he has learned it) through its completion, and

2. a strong interest in and enjoyment of young children and babies. He loves both their laughter and cries.

So how do you carve a part-time job around those skills and strengths?

James prepares two long tables for snack time at a preschool, placing tablecloths, setting out paper products, putting cookies/fruit in trays, and pouring the juice. The excitement begins when the children run in for their snack, as they are so anxious to see James. His mother says, "They laugh, call him Uncle James, and give him big hugs." James' presence at the preschool is of value to the children. Because he is there, it may be assumed that James transcends the environment in the school, changing it to a very positive experience for the children.

Although James' life is full now, unfortunately, it was not always that purposeful. His mother says that he was denied even the most basic services during the school years. School personnel wanted to hide him from other students in the general classroom setting, and refused to let him participate in school events. Her experiences revealed an uphill battle throughout the school years.

Today, James is 32 years old and is using his strengths to make preschool children happy, content, and grateful that he is there preparing their snacks. Most important, his work comes from the best he has to give and is done with enjoyment. James is making connections and friendships as well.

The people who assist him are the necessary supports that lift James to a place where he can make a community contribution. He is an excellent example of a person with a severe disability living a fuller life and being valued for his uniqueness and his contributions.

Assumptions and Doubt

Sometimes it is difficult for families and professionals to see how increasing independence or exploring a strength or gift is possible when a person's disability limitations are so evident. We have operated for so long assuming that students must first have an "acquired set of independent living skills" in order to participate fully and independently in the community. If that were true, what skills would fill a person's life?

Let's use a different analogy. Would a person buy a house if he were only allowed to see one of its rooms? Would he purchase a car if he were permitted to see only its tires? Would a person pass judgment on a book by reading only one paragraph?

The answers are "no." Good judgment requires a broader picture. Not only is that true in buying houses, cars, and books, it's true in evaluating how to live life as an adult with a disability.

Learning independent living skills is necessary, but those skills do not make an independent life complete. Establishing a quality of life with supports is critical for a person with ASD or other disabilities.

The positive examples of young adults who are already living independently show that they have succeeded by stepping up and out. With supports in place, higher levels of community participation and involvement occurred, and over time the individual surpassed many of the expectations held by families and other care providers.

When a student explores and identifies a strength or a gift, new possibilities and opportunities emerge. Unfortunately, services for adults are not mandated in every state. And, although the person may qualify for residential or vocational services, and so on, there are often long waiting lists. To further compound these problems, many service programs are still designed and operated upon beliefs lingering from years past. Programs offer clients day service involving meaningless or age-inappropriate activities. What is more, these programs are outdated and lag far behind by not using best practices and principles that reflect the knowledge gained about quality of life for individuals with disabilities.

Individuals participating in these programs or those still living at home have limited access to peers and become increasingly dependent upon others. This eventually creates a burden for everyone in the person's family. The burden eventually shifts to society. When additional funding is needed and requested, where will society decide to place it? In more sheltered programs? A better use would be to channel funds into services that offer support and empower people to attain a life of their own such as paid employment, participating in the community as consumers, and/or living in the community with self-determination and independence.

Families Offer Advice

I interviewed families to learn how they helped guide their young adult with ASD to live independently. Families candidly told me about their experiences raising their child with ASD. When employment was a goal, they talked about how important it was to find what the young adult could do best, which led to the right job.

Challenges were encountered for both the young adult and the family along the way. For many it was a difficult journey, but with diligence and perseverance, their experiences reveal to all of us how having a goal for a positive quality of life is attainable for the young adult.

All parents interviewed had young adults with ASD ranging from a diagnosis of Asperger Syndrome (high functioning) to IQs in the 20s. Growth and success did not come without obstacles or taking risks. I learned how these families took positive steps to establish independence for their young adult as well as a life for the family. Their experiences serve as great models to help other families seeking a quality of life for their young adult. Some findings are listed here.

1. Young adults exhibited a higher level of functioning across all domains of life because they had the necessary supports for employment, leisure, and living independently.

2. When the young adults' gifts and strengths were identified, they became a catalyst for integrative participation in the community.

3. Most young adults experienced challenging or traumatic events in their early 20s. Noticeable leaps in personal growth were recognized soon after that improved their lives.

4. Strong parental beliefs in independent living combined with the young adults' strengths and interests were the foundation on which they initiated supports that linked them to the community.

5. All families were active participants in creating supports that far surpassed governmental programs for the young adult.

6. Many families believed so adamantly that the young adult would live his or her own life with quality that they took risks that altered the family structure, income, and/or routines.

7. The family's quality of life and well-being improved as the young adult became less dependent upon parents (Marquette, 2007).

Developing Friendships

Everyone wants to belong in some way by having daily associates or developing friendships. Services/agencies can offer support staff to connect youth to integrative settings, but when these resources are limited, what choices remain? Showing our youth ways to develop and cultivate friendships is a struggle. We typically view their friendships as coming from within the family or the school setting. Young adults who have already left the school environment are often relegated to isolation with very limited peer social contact.

So how do we start promoting social connections among people with ASD and DD?

First, we must take steps to get the adolescent/young adult out in the community. Use a variety of combinations to start: Explore and identify the person's interests/gifts, seek environments or organizations she can participate in, recruit people you already known to become "people supports," then access areas of government resources and services. (Please refer to the Appendices for a complete list.)

Trent

Trent developed a very close friendship with his art facilitator, Elaine. She was a very gifted artist, cute, full of life and adventure. She supported and encouraged Trent during his art sessions. They developed a very unique communication system between them. Trent is revealing personal ideas and emotions to Elaine verbally and through his art in ways I never knew he was capable of.

Is their close friendship a reflection of his new self-expression? Yes, I see this relationship on a new level of Trent having his very first "best friend." Trent was in Elaine and Matt's wedding not long ago. Both Elaine and her husband, Matt, are his friends and invite Trent out for dinner and a movie on a regular basis. Elaine constantly talks about having Trent as her friend for a lifetime. All this came from Elaine and Trent working together in art.

Trent is just one of many examples showing how one's interest can connect a person to others through a support or a gift and then form a deep friendship. The key is the adolescent/young adult "stepping out" — trying something new even though it may be risky and frightening for the family. (See the Appendices for a list of strengths, gifts, areas to start the exploring and the supports to access that make developing people connections and friendships attainable.)

Leisure

Community leisure activities include having friends go to movies and sporting events with, a walk in the park, shopping, enjoying community arts programs, exercise, and so on. Support and ways to integrate youth within these leisure areas can be created through the activities in this book, as well as using the lists in the Appendices for guidance.

Typical high school graduates are out in the world doing these leisure activities, making their way and seeking to discover who they are and what they can become. Their family is involved in a limited way. But the scenario is very different when a family has a young adult with a disability. During adolescence, and especially after high school ends, the family should not be the adult's primary connection to the community. Family members work and have other responsibilities. In some cases, parents are in need of respite from the care of the adult. Young adults have a basic need to belong and participate in the community, even if they cannot express it.

A Community Coach

I realized Trent was very uneasy and insecure when all he had was me in his day. The only way I could bypass my main participation was to connect Trent to the community through someone else. I hired what I call a community coach.

What is a community coach?

A community coach is a person who introduces new activities, people, and settings to an individual with a disability within the context of the community. I found this option to be one of the most successful in increasing Trent's acceptance into the community. With a coach, Trent looked forward to working out at the YMCA, going horseback riding, shopping, and visiting the zoo. These experiences, in turn, enriched his life and provided him the confidence he needed to try new things. Most important, he moved past the stage of just tolerating a community setting to actually enjoying an activity.

How can you find a community coach?

You will not find a list of community coaches in the phone book or through an agency. I learned to let people know that I was seeking a community coach. I contacted Trent's former teacher, professionals who had helped Trent obtain services, as well as friends, neighbors, and university students. I found a wonderful college student when I accepted an invitation to speak to a university class about autism. Another time, an acquaintance referred a teacher at the private school where she worked. The answer is to get the word out to others. Network!

How do you know if a person will make a good community coach?

That is a tough question. However, I found certain guidelines that helped me make a decision to hire a person. I looked for someone who

- was referred to me and agreed to undergo a background check and provided references I could call

- had some past experience with an individual who has a disability, although this should not be a requirement (some of the better coaches were people who did not know anything about autism)

- understood and valued the community as a way to open up the world for a person with a disability

- had a car and insurance

Some of you may be saying, "But my son/daughter has too many behavioral issues to use a community coach." I know from experience that Trent and other young adults had many issues in managing appropriate behavior as well. There were times when I could not handle Trent's issues in public by myself, and I consequently stopped taking him out alone. But through the support of a community coach, Trent's life changed from total isolation in the home and drowning in obsessive behaviors to a life of community activities: painting his world as he sees it, going horseback riding, working at his job in the lawn and garden center at a large retail store, and experiencing new and different situations that once I only dreamed of seeing.

There is a basic theory of expectation: *If we are told that we are different often enough, we start believing it.* When Trent saw how others wanted to help him and accept him, he believed it and became more comfortable exploring new possibilities. Essentially, he began to believe what others believed about his ability.

Employment

The goal for many individuals with disabilities is to become employed, not just anywhere, but in an environment with tasks that match their strengths. In *Developing Talents* geared for individuals who are higher functioning, Grandin and Duffy (2004) offer useful tips for developing skills that can be channeled into fields such as computers, engineering, designing, and journalism.

For others who may have more involved disabilities, establishing supports that meet the individual's needs is essential. The WP process can guide the search for the right job. These are the steps I recommend:

1. Work through the activities and the process in Chapter Four completely.

2. Determine the individual's strengths and gifts along with his or her needs. Naming the individual's needs will determine the supports that must be established for employment success.

3. Take time to evaluate and review all insights from doing the activities.

The steps to follow are critical. Let's suppose you hear that a new Wal-Mart is hiring in town. You are tempted to rush in and seek a job for the young adult you are working with. WRONG!

Let me explain. There is a very important question to ask first that will lead you on the right path. Take the list of strengths and gifts in hand along with the person's needs and ask:

What would have to happen for Juan to become successfully employed using his gift of _____ and having the supports _____ to meet his need_____?

Example:

What would have to happen for Juan to become successfully employed using his gift of *organizing and memorizing information well* and having the supports from a *coworker, or mentor, and a visual display* to meet his needs *of understanding the social rules of the business and knowing who to ask for help?*

Brainstorm a variety of tasks, settings, and areas where Juan could know success with these supports. This is best done with a team as a support. For instance, invite the young adult's Vocational Rehabilitation counselor, teachers, a potential provider agency in supported employment, and/or other interested persons such as neighbors, friends of family, and so on. Encourage team members to be open and to freely suggest options. Let go of any rigid presupposed ideas. Leave room for surprise suggestions or options that have never been considered.

Jobs are carved every day. If a job description does not meet the person's ability to carry out all the tasks, modify it and create a new job. I was part of the process with others who found students jobs using this process. Remember, this is a creative action-oriented process that requires effort and loyalty of a group of people who have the person's well-being in mind.

Establishing Employment and Necessary Supports — An Example

This creative process worked for Trent in each job he had. I will use Trent as an example, mainly because I am most familiar with his needs and the sensibilities of being a parent and working through the process.

It was my goal since he was very young that Trent would live independently and have a job after high school. When high school ended, he was confronted with traumatic change all around him, to include parental separation and divorce, brothers leaving home for work or college, moving to a new residence, and losing three jobs within the first year.

Then the ultimate crisis hit him. In the midst of creating independent living, I moved out and Jason, his new roommate, moved in. These changes led to extreme resistance. Trent became even more obsessive and compulsive and withdrew from everyone and everything. He was very depressed. Jason and I worked together and provided the support Trent needed in order to overcome the challenges. We purposely took Trent to different community settings each day (grocery store, library, the park, etc.). Each time Trent locked himself into an obsession by moving an item around on a store shelf or was unable to move because he was obsessing on arranging a stick on the sidewalk in the park, we helped push him past the obsession. We became his support, and gently took him arm in arm, escorting him out of the setting, thereby unlocking his obsession.

With continual daily practice, Trent became less resistant and began to trust that with all the changes happening in his life, he was still O.K. He learned that I had not completely left him. He accepted that his family didn't live with him any more, and discovered that I was around and fully there for him when he needed me. He was not able to communicate through sentences how he was feeling, but he indicated it through his body language, which was more and more relaxed. He became receptive to engage in activities and living with Jason — he had begun accepting his new life.

After Trent had lived independently for four months, still recovering from the trauma, my intuition told me this was the time to help him seek a job that would keep him moving forward as much as possible. At the time I was working as a consultant in a local school district. The job coaches and I were establishing "paid" jobs for students with disabilities. One of our students at a local retail store was hired to pull plastic off clothes and place shoes in boxes for sale on the floor. As soon as I saw that task, I knew that Trent could do it. It was repetitive and matched his strengths and his ability to follow through with all the steps of a task. I also knew that this job, which was in the back of the store away from the public, would be ideal for him because when he had a setback, there would not be a scene in front of customers.

The regional manager was also the manager of the Kmart stores in Louisville where we lived. I called and requested a time to meet with him about hiring a person with autism. He met with all of us, Trent, myself, Troy, Trent's job coach, and Barry, the director of Community Employment, a provider in supported employment. After the regional manager heard about

Trent's capabilities along with his needs, he recommended that we meet with a manager in a particular store and promptly set up a meeting.

Our next meeting was with the store manager and the department team leader over clothing. The persons attending the meeting included the two managers at Kmart, myself, Barry, and Troy. The store managers gave us a tour through the clothing department, showing us the various job tasks. Barry quickly jumped in and made comments about Trent's capabilities, but also his needs. He suggested that a job be carved in which Trent would place security tags on clothing. He also made some requests. For example, he said, that Trent might need to have time away from his task to calm down when he became upset; he might have a bad day and need to go home early occasionally; he would need to have one particular task to do in one particular area; he would need a maximum of 10 hours of work per week starting off. Finally, he said that Trent would need to have people supports and requested that Jason and Trent be hired as a team. To my surprise, the managers agreed to all of it; in fact, they were excited to try it. I was exceedingly amazed and grateful for their openness and willingness. Trent and Jason worked at Kmart for the next 15 months. It was a great job for Trent.

The job ended when the store downsized all stores across the country. I dreaded it, but I began the process of looking for another job. At that time, we had already taken plenty of photos and even a video of Trent working in all phases of his job. We went to another retail store, Meijer. How did I choose that store? This is where networking comes in so wonderfully. I attended my family reunion in Battle Creek, Michigan, and learned that my cousin was a manager of one of the very first Meijer stores built. On my request, he made a phone call to a manager in our town to set up a meeting to discuss Trent's employment.

Troy, the job coach, and I met with the manager, explained Trent's capabilities, and handed him a video of Trent working. The store manager saw how capable Trent was with Jason's support as a coworker. Trent and Jason were again hired as a team. Trent has worked 20 hours a week in the Pet Department now for over five years. A few months ago, he was awarded a certificate for five years of dedicated service. Most important, he has grown beyond our expectations. Although both Jason and Trent still work at Meijer, Trent works completely independently and with other coworkers, rotating to other departments the last two hours of his shift. Jason works in another department.

Many other individuals with disabilities, whether mild or severe, have used the job carving process and coworker supports to maintain jobs that became good matches. The dreams that youth have and we have for them can be realized. Most important, the chance to have a dream for something, and then live it, can become a reality.

Building Employment Supports

Below I offer two examples of young adults, Phillip and Patrick, working at a job with supports to maintain employment.

Phillip's Story. Phillip has Asperger Syndrome and is high functioning. He works at a large retail store where he stocks shelves and hauls in carts from the parking lot. One particular day, his team leader asked him to help coworkers unload trucks because the store was short of staff. Phillip had never done this before and did not know the coworkers, but he did what he was asked to do. After the trucks were unloaded, two coworkers left the area. Phillip stood there alone with no other task to do and assumed that it was alright to leave just as the two other coworkers had done. He had only 15 minutes left on his shift, so he went out to the parking lot and walked the perimeter of the entire property of the business, using up the 15 minutes the best way he knew.

The next day, the manager called his dad and informed him that Phillip would be denied a day of work as punishment. Phillip was excited about having a day off. Dad asked Phillip about the situation and why he had left the area. Phillip responded that after the guys left, he followed the store's rule by staying and just walking the property lot. This made sense to him.

What was happening here? The manager perceived Phillip's response to the situation as defiance when that was not his intention. Phillip was unable to predict that the choice he made would be viewed as defiance when he kept to the rule he understood, staying on the property the last 15 minutes.

In this case, Phillip's dad is his mentor and support. Dad met with the manager and explained how Phillip recognized the social rule to stay on the property and remain for the exact time required. He requested that Phillip get support to understand the manager's point of view and perspective. Phillip had difficulty understanding the cause and effect of a decision as well as predicting outcomes. That is, he was unable to predict that walking the perimeter for the last 15 minutes was not following the rules.

When job tasks change, his dad suggested that Phillip may need extra support and a detailed explanation to understand what is expected. His dad conveyed that a day of work withheld was not seen as a punishment by Phillip. The manager appreciated the information, yet he chose to follow through with his decision.

Patrick's Story. Patrick, who also has Asperger Syndrome, worked at a grocery store successfully for nearly five years. The job supported his living in an apartment and paying his own bills. He stocked shelves and worked in Customer Service bagging groceries and escorting people to their cars. After four years, the management changed, and in the process Patrick was separated from some coworkers with whom he had enjoyed working.

Patrick began telling his mother that some of the new coworkers were laughing at him and he did not understand why. A few months later Patrick was demoted. The new manager limited his work tasks to only bagging groceries. Patrick quit his job abruptly one day. He could not give his mother any reason why he was demoted or why he wanted to quit.

Patrick has a hard time finding the words that express his feelings and concerns. He also has difficulty reading people's faces and body language, takes comments literally, and does not understanding sarcasm. His mother wanted to meet with the new manager, but Patrick asked her not to.

In this case, Patrick's job may have been saved if a mentor or support person had been available to explain some of his characteristics, which reflect having Asperger Syndrome. He clearly had success with the previous manager, who was able to understand his challenges with nonverbal communication. At times Patrick may need a manager or mentor who can provide frequent feedback that is positive, encouraging, and literal about job tasks. When significant changes occur, he could use the support of someone explaining what is happening and what that means for him. Possibly, the previous coworkers understood the supports that Patrick needed and provided them naturally.

Perhaps his coworkers understood the changes that were happening with the new management and Patrick didn't receive that feedback for some reason. Having had someone explain to him why his job was changing would have opened up a discussion about his work tasks, the past five years of excellent work ethic, and the possibility of continuing previous job tasks as well as learn new ones.

(Refer to Appendix E for other examples of students who attained work through job carving and natural supports.)

At times, it appears the needs of people with ASD are overwhelming. Yet, when offered tasks they can do, and with the needed supports, they can give the best they have. Awareness and understanding are the keys here.

Reframed Thinking

When someone makes a positive comment about Trent's independent living or art success, I hear myself thinking, "I am happy and proud of Trent's accomplishments." Yet, a part of me wants to race ahead with apprehension and say, "But what if he stops painting? What if he regresses and no one accepts him again?" But those questions will lead me down the wrong path. Focusing on the goal and nothing else is the solution. Parents are vulnerable to the young adult's activities. I learned that I became less vulnerable each time I encouraged Trent to step out into a new area.

As advocates, we may think that guiding a young adult into self-exploration requires a lot of time and effort. How does a parent or advocate find time to do it all? I still struggle with the time issue; yet, I developed a new perspective about it. Imagine that we have a "creative/emotional" bank account. I will use myself as an example. My creative emotional bank account has $100.00 in it. Let's say $55.00 was spent on protecting Trent from outside experiences based on previous failures. Thirty dollars was spent on worrying about how others saw Trent initiating a new activity. All I have left is $15.00 to spend on doing my best creative emotional work in guiding my son. That is not much to invest in guiding my son. I have been there. I am advocating something I once agonized over. The trick is to gather and direct all our creative emotional dollars in the same direction. When I chose effort and focus on Trent' strengths, gifts, and community participation, I had less time for overprotection and worry.

Taking risks requires that we contradict our past assumptions and beliefs about our relationships with our young adult. It requires that we reframe our thinking. Taking calculated and necessary risks despite uncertainty is where strength lies that can lead your youth to a life of purpose and personal growth.

There is a saying that a boat may be safe when it's in harbor, but that isn't what boats were made for. Boats were made to sail. The same goes for people with disabilities. They are made to sail and live their lives expressed uniquely as their own, as persons with value. Seeking new experiences, meeting new people, living life to its fullest are some of the best reasons for being alive.

Your son or daughter may be safe at home or content in a day program. All seems well now because the functional purposes for these programs are often viewed as safe harbors. The truth is that youth who are languishing in day programs or at home are often living well below their capabilities.

If you are using a day service, I encourage you to start where you are and consider other ways of involvement for the young adult. Try to see other options that can expand his capability and connections to others. My son participated in disability programs as well. I learned not to place all of my hopes, dependency, and dreams for his quality of life in just one program. Begin now, take a small step and seek help for the young adult to explore interests/gifts through peer support and involvement in community settings.

View a day program as a temporary harbor, while you guide your daughter or son to explore creative options a little more each day. Seek professionals who have beliefs that offer support to help individuals explore their strengths and gifts *within inclusive settings*. Each person has a different level of capability and unique needs. As a parent, occasionally push your adolescent/young adult's limits to reach higher capability levels in one setting at a time. Each time you try, you will be giving him a chance to experience growth and change.

Equate safe harbors with programs that are resting places as you catch your breath, contemplate, and then move forward to the next place. DO not use these harbors as the one and only way to get by. With your consistent, conscious effort and collaboration with professionals, one day your son or daughter may have gained the strength and support to live more fully in the community.

Professionals and Parents — Collaboration

School personnel, policymakers, and parents are faced with the challenge to address the needs of the enormous flux of students with disabilities entering adult life. Some are simply ignoring the issues. There has been a national crisis for adults with developmental disabilities for over a decade.

What power do young adults and families have? Is the only answer advocating for increased sheltered programs that isolate our youth? What if the young adult and families want more, a chance to participate, grow, and live in the community?

One thing is certain. Before funding sheltered programs, we as a society need to view the individual's basic needs from *his* perspective. The WP model offers a unique solution and places a map of empowerment into the hands of the individual, the family, the professionals, and the community.

Agencies and schools cannot provide full quality of life to persons with disabilities. These systems are designed to serve a great number of individuals with diverse needs. They are limited in knowing well what any one individual needs, functionally and emotionally. Much more is needed, and much more is required. If we gauge our support to youth with disabilities as only teaching independent skills, that makes our relationships with them superficial. They need us to listen, observe, and involve them to become more emotionally self-accepting and self-directed.

Much has been written about assisting individuals who are high functioning. But what about persons who have labels of low functioning? To address this issue was one reason why I wrote this book. I wanted to offer helpful information that is inclusive, regardless of the level of disability.

Experts and parents question whether individuals who are labeled low functioning can do self-exploratory activities. Some may ask, "Is that teachable? Can students really self-explore when faced with so many challenges?"

A student's IEP lists his or her interests and strengths. Yet, we do not do enough in implementing action plan around the student's gifts. Independent living skills are taught in isolated settings and in bits and pieces. When the individual accomplishes all the steps, she is awarded a certificate indicating that she can now clean house, cook a meal, bathe herself, and even use the phone for an emergency. Through evaluation we have determined she has earned the right to live in a group home or an apartment independently or with assistance.

Have we done all we can to help her ensure her independent living is a success? Not if we fail to include the necessary supports that enable her to offer her best gifts and strengths at work and at leisure. When we leave out all that makes life worth living, we have overemphasized "independent living skills" and have taught with detachment.

We have left out preparing her psychologically and emotionally for adult living.

True self-expression and true living requires true honesty. This means that our youth with disabilities must experience vulnerability to grow. This includes facing failure, trying again when he/she feels excluded, and responding at basic levels of responsibility. You might think that sounds harsh. But I have left something important out: The student does not do this all alone, or in a vacuum, completely independently. Experts have written that the individual must be independent, on one's own, but that is not completely true.

He does it "with supports" that we — the advocates — help create.

Once the individual with a disability puts himself "out there," he is rendered vulnerable. As advocates, we allow fear to set in and worry about the outcome. There is truth to fearing the outcome, but the greater truth has been a well-kept secret. Here are some examples of the greater truth.

Once the person puts her effort/gift/contribution "out there," she becomes a little less vulnerable. What she has created is a piece of turf on which she is willing to stand; for example, a favorite leisure activity where she makes friends; a job that is a good match to her strengths; or an apartment she is responsible for keeping clean. Her contribution may include providing a viable task for a job (stocking shelves in a grocery store), being a member of a church choir, filing papers in a clerk's office (for pay), or attending an art opening where she, the artist, will be recognized. All these examples reveal the essence of living a life with purpose.

As educators, we care deeply about our work. We know well that there are resource shortages for serving people with disabilities. One significant way schools can help students is to offer the tools to continue pursuing gifts and creating supports that help students attain a life live with daily purpose. School personnel will benefit from these techniques that have helped many other students and their families.

Families are the foundation of support, and their role as a guide for the young adult is significantly increased during transition. Who other than the family has a vested interest in ensuring a quality of life for the young adult? Many parents have expressed in desperate voices that they want to help their young adult but do not know what to do. School personnel play a vital role in collaborating with families to share information about services and approaches that can assist in the young adult's growth and independence. This is an area that is largely missing from transition plans and programs.

Here are some suggestions for collaboration efforts involving professionals and parents:

- Start the WP process in early adolescence.

- Offer activities that build self-acceptance and self-worth by exploring and using strengths. The activities are designed to help youth take responsibility in pursuing the process.

- Provide activities and strategies that assist the adolescents/young adult and their families in a self-assessment and exploration process that reveal interests, gifts, and talents.

- Conduct the exploration process to identify interest and talents during school. This will better enable the student with the family's help to negotiate life after high school.

- Change the focus of assessment from deficits to capability building based on support and assistance.

- Offer new measurement tools that assess students' capability in living.

In summary, the WP model can guide the adolescent/young adult (with collaboration from family and professionals) to negotiate a life that becomes uniquely his or her own. The activities presented here lead to the recognition of numerous possibilities for creating supports that make community participation real during adolescence and adulthood.

The hurried pace with which most of us live today places demands on persons with ASD and DD as well as the family to exhibit appropriate behavior at all times, meet academic expectations, and tolerate the external forces that require one to "fit in." The goal to fit in that we advocates work so hard to help our youth achieve can cause youth to feel empty and draw our attention away from seeing their true gifts. Having basic skills is essential, but the development of those skills alone does not make a person's life. Our youth must also learn the emotional skills of life that establish self-acceptance, purpose, and value.

Approaches and programs that emphasize our youth's involvement and acceptance in all areas of living are desperately needed. Professionals and advocates must be positive risk takers. Together we can help adolescents and young adults collect pieces of the best they have to give. Most important, let's encourage the development of disability policy that offers "supports" that empower youth to step out and soar through the transition years attaining a life of their own.

AFTERWORD

Trent is now 30 years old. As I have been advocating on his behalf for years, I want to end at the beginning. When Trent was 3 years old, I received a brochure from an agency in Maryland that provided community living and employment to adults with autism. Reading that information gave me hope at a time when I was still in shock about the autism diagnosis. Holding the brochure in my hands was one of the things that planted my first seed of hope. It also inspired the passion later to take the leap toward Trent's independence and to help him discover his purpose in life. The sentiment of that event still resonates with me. I am not sure what the next chapter of our lives will hold for Trent and me or how our dreams will evolve, but I do know that I look forward to it with the same spirit of adventure.

I discovered the path to this dream is not straight. Trent and I got lost, but eventually we found our way back. It is okay to change direction, and it is never too late to start. If you think your adolescent/young adult wants meaningful employment, then be determined to ask for help and find it. If you have always known how beautifully your daughter sang, but you think that she may not be accepted or hurt if turned down at an audition, encourage her any way.

Along the way, I have experienced many highs and lows. The hard work to create independence can be overwhelming. During the trying times, the stress seemed to seep into every cell of my body and soul. During the high points, anything seemed possible. There were several times along the way when I wanted to give up and found myself questioning what I was really gaining besides stress and tension. Pushing myself, with the fear of facing unknown challenges, never knowing the outcome of something new, can cause any sane person to wonder if it is all worth it. Creating a meaningful life for our young adults who have disabilities is worth it. Following our hearts, embracing our passions, and encouraging our young adults to live their lives is worth every bit of the pain and courage it requires.

When I see my son's growth, vigor (expressed through painting), and general confidence in social settings that used to evoke public scenes and seemingly endless obsessions, I find strength. When I hear stories of how others have overcome similar obstacles, I find power and courage to keep going. We must dare to encourage our children to dream and to express their individuality.

References

Beattie, M. (1987). *Codependent no more*. San Francisco: Harper Collins Publishers.

Berkowitz, E. D. (1996). History of self-determination. In D. J. Sands & M. L. Wehmeyer (Eds.), *Self-determination across the lifespan: Independence and choice for people with disabilities* (pp. 3-5). Baltimore: Paul H. Brookes.

Blue-Banning, M., & Turnbull, A. P. (2002). Hispanic youth/young adults with disabilities: Parents' visions for the future. *Research & Practice for Persons with Severe Disabilities, 27,* 204-219.

Callahan, M. J., & Garner, J. B. (Eds.). (1997). *Keys to the workplace: Skills and supports for people with disabilities*. Baltimore: Paul H. Brookes.

CDC Media Relations Press Release. (2007, February 8). *CDC releases new data on autism spectrum disorders (ASDs) from multiple communities in the United States*. Retrieved March 25, 2007, from http://www.cdc.gov/od/oc/media/pressrel/2007/r07208.htm

Covert, S. (1992). Supporting families. In J. Nisbet (Ed.), *Natural supports in school, at work, and in the community for people with severe disabilities* (pp. 121-162). Baltimore: Paul H. Brookes.

Dunst, C. J., Trivette, C. M., Gordon, J. J., & Pletcher, L. L. (1989). Building and mobilizing informal family support networks. In G.H.S. Singer & L. K. Irvin (Eds.), *Support for caregiving families: Enabling positive adaptation to disability* (pp. 121-141). Baltimore: Paul H. Brookes Publishing.

Education for All Handicapped Children Act of 1975, P. L. 94-142, 20 U.S.C. § 1401 *et seq.*

Ferguson, P. M., Ferguson, D., & Jones, D. (1988). Generations of hope: Parental perspectives on the transitions of their children with severe retardation from school to adult life. *Journal of the Association for persons with Severe Handicaps, 13,* 177-187.

Gerber, R. (2002). *Leadership the Eleanor Roosevelt way.* New York: Prentice Hall Press.

Gilman, C. (1997). *Doing work you love.* Chicago: Contemporary Books.

Gray, D. E., & Holden, W. J. (1992). Psycho-social well-being among the parents of children with autism. *Australia and New Zealand Journal of Developmental Disabilities, 18*(2), 83-93.

Grandin, T., & Duffy, K. (2004). *Developing talents — Careers for individuals with Asperger Syndrome and high-functioning autism.* Shawnee Mission, KS: Autism Asperger Publishing Company.

Greenspan, S., & Wieder, S. (1998). *The child with special needs: Encouraging intellectual and emotional growth.* Cambridge, MA: Da Capo Press.

Greenspan, I., & Wieder, S. (2006). *Engaging autism: Using the floor time approach to help children relate, communicate, and think.* Cambridge, MA: Da Capo Lifelong Books.

Hayden, M. F., Spicer, P., Depaepe, P., & Chelberg, G. (1992). Waiting for community services: Support and service needs of families with adult members with mental retardation and other developmental disabilities. *Policy Research Brief, 4*(4), 1-12.

Individuals with Disabilities Education Act of 1990, Pub. L. No. 101-476, 20 U.S.C. § 1400 *et seq.* (1990).

Kantrowitz, B., & Scelfo, J. (2006, November). *Growing up with autism.* Retrieved February 5, 2007, from http://www.msnbc.msn.com/id/15792805/site/newsweek

Kosciulek, J. F. (1999). The consumer-directed theory of empowerment. *Rehabilitation Counseling Bulletin, 42,* 196-213.

Konstantereas, M., Homatidis, S., & Plowright, C.M.S. (1992). Assessing resources and stress in parents of severely dysfunctional children. *Journal of Autism and Developmental Disorders, 22,* 217-234.

Mallory, B. L. (1995). The role of social policy on life-cycle transitions. *Exceptional Children, 62,* 213-223.

Marquette, J. M. (2001). *Independence bound: A mother and her autistic son's journey to adulthood.* Louisville, KY: Harmony House Publishing.

Marquette, J. M. (2007). *Autism and post-high school transition to community assisted living: Parental perceptions.* Manuscript in preparation, University of Louisville, Louisville, KY.

Marquette, J. M., & Miller, S. K. (2002, October). *Autism and transition to independent living: Exploring changes in family functioning.* Paper presented at the annual conference of the Association of University Centers on Disabilities, Bethesda, MD.

Marquette, J. M., & Miller, S. K. (2004, November/December). Remarkably able: Transition to independent assisted living. *Autism Asperger's Digest,* 36-39.

Meyer, R. J. (1980). Attitudes of parents of institutionalized mentally retarded individuals toward deinstitutionalization. *American Journal of Mental Deficiency, 85,* 478-488.

Mcloughlin, C. S., Garner, J. B., & Callahan, M. J. (1987). *Getting employed, staying employed.* Baltimore: Paul H. Brookes.

Morningstar, M. E., Turnbull, A. P., & Turnbull, H. R. (1995). What do students with disabilities tell us about the importance of family involvement in transition from school to adult life? *Exceptional Children, 62,* 249-260.

Mount, B. (2000). *Life building: Opening windows for change, using personal futures planning.* Armenia, NY: Capacity Works.

Prizant, B., & Wetherby A. M. (1998). Understanding the continuum of discrete-trial traditional behavioral to social-pragmatic developmental approaches in communication enhancement for young children with autism/PDD. *Seminars in Speech and Language, 19,* 329-353.

Sarason, S. B., & Doris, J. (1979). Social system perspective. In S. J. Vitello & R. M. Soskin (Eds.), *Mental retardation: Its social and legal context* (pp. 13-15). Englewood Cliffs, NJ: Prentice-Hall.

Schuster, J. L., Timmons, J. C., & Moloney, M. (2003). Barriers to successful transition for young adults who receive SSI and their families. *Career Development for Exceptional Individuals, 26,* 47-66.

Seligman, M. (2005a). *Authentic happiness: Using the new psychology to realize your potential for lasting fulfillment.* New York: Free Press.

Seligman, M. (2005b). Keynote address at the National Annual School Psychologists Convention, Atlanta, GA.

Seligman, M. (2006). *Learned optimism: How to change your mind and your life* (3rd ed.). New York: Vintage Books.

Sharpley, C. F., Bitsika, V., & Efremidis, B. (1997). Influence of gender, parental health, and perceived expertise of assistance upon stress, anxiety, and depression among parents of children with autism. *Journal of Intellectual & Developmental Disability, 22,* 19-28.

Singer, G. S., & Irvin, L. K. (1991). Supporting families of persons with severe disabilities: Emerging findings, practices, and questions. In L. H. Meyer, C. A. Peck, & L. L. Brown (Eds.), *Critical issues in the lives of people with severe disabilities* (pp. 271-305). Baltimore: Paul H. Brookes.

Stancliffe, R. J., & Parmenter T. R. (1999). The Choice Questionnaire: A scale to Assess choices exercised by adults with intellectual disability. *Journal of Intellectual & Developmental Disability, 24,* 107-132.

Stein, J. (1997). *Empowerment and women's health.* Atlantic Highlands, NJ: Zed Books, Ltd.

Sullivan, R. (2001, June 20). *Autism Society of America position paper on the national crisis of adult services for individuals with autism.* Retrieved October 1, 2002, from http://www.autismservices.com/position.pdf

Taylor, S. J. (1987). Introduction. In D. Taylor & J. K. Biklen (Eds.), *Community integration for people with severe disabilities* (pp. xv-xx). New York: Teachers College Press.

Taylor, S. J., Bogdan, R., & Racino, J. A. (1991). Conclusion. In S. J. Taylor, R. Bogdan, & J. A. Racino (Eds.), *Life in the community: Case studies of organizations supporting people with disabilities* (pp. 253-258). Baltimore: Paul H. Brookes.

Turnbull, A. P., Blue-Banning, M. J., Anderson, E. L., Turnbull, H. R., Seaton, K. A., & Dinas, P. A. (1996). Enhancing self-determination through group action planning. In D. J. Sands & M. L. Wehmeyer (Eds.), *Self-determination across the life span: Independence and choice for people with disabilities* (pp. 237-256). Baltimore: Paul H. Brookes.

Vitello, S. J., & Soskin, R. M. (1985). *Mental retardation: Its social and legal context*. Englewood Cliffs, NJ: Prentice-Hall.

Ward, M. (1996). Coming of age in the age of self-determination. In D. J. Sands & M. L. Wehmeyer (Eds.), *Self-determination across the life span: Independence and choice for people with disabilities* (pp. 3-36). Baltimore: Paul H. Brookes.

Wing, L. (2001). *The autistic spectrum: A parent's guide to understanding and helping your child*. Berkeley, CA: Ulysses Press.

Zaks, Z. (2006). *Life and love: Positive strategies for autistic adults*. Shawnee Missions, KS: Autism Aspergers Publishing Company.

APPENDIX A

Our Family's Journey

Picture a bridge. On one side of the bridge, it is cold and dark. Adults with disabilities and their families lived there in isolation. Our family stood with all the others. Some of us kept our child at home after graduation, protecting them from the harsh world. Worse, some individuals went to live in restrictive settings, separated from loved ones because of emergencies, such as illness or death of parents. These were once considered our only options.

A few professionals who worked in the field began promoting independence for people with disabilities. Yet other professionals and lawmakers hesitated to change policies to support community living for adults with disabilities. They weren't willing to change. "Persons with disabilities aren't capable of community life. It's not possible. It will cost too much. There are no jobs for these individuals," was the message. Ultimately, families became distracted by their pain and accepted their lives, saying, "This is the way it is, and this is the way it always will be."

Then some of us got lucky. Our eyes opened, through the grace of God, because it was time. Trent and I wanted to believe there was a bridge leading us to a new shore. We decided to go alone, because we heard a few people on the other side cheering us onward. We didn't know the way, so we journeyed blindly, taking one small step at a time. The closer we got to the other side, the more we could see, and feel, that what we had been promised was real. As we arrived, we discovered there was support, acceptance, and a place to live, belong, and grow.

We began telling others how wonderful our life had become. We tried to convince others still standing on the cliff that there was a bridge to a better place. Some listened. Many refused to see the bridge. Others didn't want to believe it. They were afraid. They were not yet ready for the journey.

But now there is a bridge. We found it. So have numerous other families, although those who have crossed it are still the exceptions. Those still on the other side CAN find the bridge, with help and encouragement. Sometimes, those of us who have made it are tempted to go back and drag others over with us, but this won't work. Each family must chart their own journey. No one can be forced across the bridge. Each young adult, each family must go by choice. When the time is right, some will come; some may stay on the other side.

Trent and I can help guide them. We can wave to them. We can shout back and forth. We can cheer them on just as others have cheered and encouraged us. But we cannot insist they come over with us.

We have already crossed the bridge and are standing here in the afterglow of independence and inclusion. It is our chance to live our lives and know acceptance. But the journey was difficult. At times, we didn't think we would ever make it across. We do not have to feel guilty now or even fearful. It is where we are meant to be. We do not have to go back to the dark cliff. We can let go of our fear of the past.

Trent and I choose to continue walking our path and reassuring others that there is a better place. We are committed to helping. Although other young adults and their families must decide to cross the bridge to independent living, their journey need not be isolated. Helping these families take advantage of what I have learned about resources, processes, and overcoming barriers is what this workbook is all about. And Trent and I will be right there to cheer them on, just as others did for us.

Jackie M. Marquette

Appendix B

Gifts, Talents, Strengths, and Interests

Seligman (2005) defines and differentiates strengths and talents.

Talent is innate. Examples of talent include singing with perfect pitch, running at lightning speed, and painting beautiful pieces on a canvas. Talent involves choices, such as whether to develop it. A person does not have a choice to possess it.

Strengths are usually more voluntary. Having a strength in an area involves choosing when to use it and whether to keep building upon it. For example, telling the cashier that he undercharged you $5.00 is personal strength and a decision to apply it. Thus, strengths can be built upon with time and effort.

Below are lists of talents and strengths. These qualities may be found in individuals with ASD and DD.

Gifts and Talents

Individuals with ASD have been known to:
- have strong visual thinking skills
- be able to categorize
- have increased understanding and appreciation for rules and systems
- be able to concentrate intensely
- handle concrete tasks, learning things one step at a time
- be knowledgeable about a topical interest
- retain large amounts of facts
- have original, interesting reactions to the typical, ordinary ways of the world
- use unique ways to resolve problems
- make others laugh or smile (not ridicule, but smiling or laughing to relate or tell jokes)
- be entertaining — could be anything; some examples comedian or singer
- make people and things beautiful, such as arranging: flowers
- listen to favorite kind of music (learning information about groups, musicians, modern and classical, jazz, blues, etc.)
- sing in choir, chorus, in church, community organization
- play an instrument
- enjoy concerts (school, community organizations) (giving appreciation to others as an audience member)
- be artistic (craft, sculpting, pottery, painting)
- read maps well (serve others, help others)
- memorize information well
- use unique life experiences to benefit others
- communicate in their own unique style (i.e., singing, artistic creations)
- be good at problem solving
- engage in thinking that makes sense from the point of view of the person, mathematical thinking, numbers, time, dates, calendars
- write
- arrange pieces into a whole, for example putting a bicycle together
- create something from nothing (e.g., build sand castles or make art from various media)
- organize
- teach a task to someone else
- have style — the person's unique style that makes his or her gift original. A unique personality that shines as the person approaches a task or job.
- be intelligent
- be knowledgeable
- have physical strength
- inspire or motivate others

Strengths

- helping others
- comforting others
- being loyal
- using charts, developing lists, following rules
- enjoying quiet and calm
- hope
- courage
- honesty

- kindness
- curiosity, interest in the world
- love of learning about a topic of interest
- open-mindedness
- perspective
- perseverance
- humanity and love
- loving and allowing oneself to be loved
- good citizenship
- fairness and equity
- humility and modesty
- transcendence
- appreciation of beauty and excellence
- gratitude
- hope and optimism
- spirituality
- sense of purpose
- forgiveness
- zest, passion, and enthusiasm

Interests

Academics (math, etc.)
Watching videos
Bike rides
Playing games
Playing Computer games
Educational events
Skiing
Tae kwon do
Hockey
Chess
Astronomy
Mythology
Science fiction
History
Biography
Picnics
Hiking
Fishing
Horseback riding
Rowing
Swimming
Weight training
Community festivals
Classes (adult education)
Caring for animals (Humane Society)
Environment preservation (wildlife)
Health issues (Red Cross)

Appendix C

Supports/Assistance

Questions to Ask When Seeking Supports to Explore an Adolescent/Young Adult's Strengths and Gifts:
- What environmental settings are difficult for him to enter?
- What is his level of tolerating the sensory issues within a certain environment?
- What conditions does he prefer?
- Does he have any sensory issues that need preparation for in advance?
- What supports can decrease disruptions or distractions?
- What supports could help prioritize tasks?
- What are some soothing and calming techniques that have worked to buffer sensory issues within a setting?

Technical Supports and Strategies

Visual supports are an excellent resource when teaching new routines as they enhance understanding of routine and create independence. Examples include:
- Visual pictures, drawings, photographs
- Color coding (e.g., colored tape highlighters to assist in communication, enhance learning)
- Pictures or written list revealing the steps in a routine (e.g., use a story map to steps in checking out a library book, brushing teeth)
- Calendar of monthly events and appointments
- Visual schedules of daily routines and monthly events

- Simple pictorial representation of a series of activities or tasks
- Pictures or icons of objects/events
- Pictures or icons to assist in understanding of receptive language
- Checklists of activities or chores
- Calming techniques (breathing deeply, a safe place to regain balance, Walkman with calm music to drown out noise and confusion)
- Light sensitivity (sunglasses an option)
- Photos or video of person participating in an activity or managing something new
- Social Stories™ to handle difficult situations as well as to note accomplishments (books and other information are readily available on this topic)

People Supports — Ideas for Creating Supports Among Others

People supports are crucial to entering particular environments and participating actively.
- Student/peer helper
- Immediate and extended family members (although this is often difficult)
- Support coordinator
- Job coach
- Therapists/physicians
- Neighbors
- Church socials, Bible study mate
- Peer/coach who supports the youth's interest and becomes a friend: bowling partner, workout buddy at the YMCA, volunteer assistant with a service organization.
- Community coach/mentor
- Coworker support on the job
- Housemate
- Extended family members
- Bible study teacher
- Assistant in classroom (in school)
- Volunteer peer assistant (in school)
- Friends of family and friends of siblings

People supports can help the individual participate in community or integrated settings. For example, they can
- help determine why a behavior occurs
- help identify stress in the individual
- empathize with the pressure the person is experiencing
- model appropriate responses to stress
- guide the individual to relax
- teach deep breathing techniques
- teach medication
- encourage the individual and validate the person's fears
- offer consistent skill training within the environment

Appendix D

Programs and Organizations

Below is a list of programs and organizations where social connections and friendships may be made.

Service Organizations
>Adult learning classes held in local schools
Programs affiliated with museums and libraries
Patriotic organizations
Civic education organizations
Hobby and special interest groups
Character-building organizations
Political organizations
Religious organizations
Sports organizations
Ethnic heritage groups
Self help groups
Community festivals
Caring for animals (Humane Society)
Environment preservation (Wildlife)
Health issues (Red Cross)

Service Clubs in Schools
Interact Club (Rotary International)
Key Club (Kiwanis International)
Leo Club (Lions Clubs International)
Boys club
Boy Scouts
Girl Scouts
Habitat for Humanity
United Way of America

Environments
Theatres
Museums
Shops
Restaurants
Church
Parks (camping)
Schools
Farm
Neighborhood festivals/fund-raisers
Community musical festivals
Art fairs
Retreats
YMCA
Gym

Appendix E:

Successful Paid Employment (Examples)

Student	Challenges	Setbacks	Exploration	Outcome
Alex Has Traumatic Brain Injury and is legally blind. Had an injury at two years of age when a tree fell on him. He is now 20 years old. Always happy and positive. (+) Eager to try new things (+). Wears a leg brace. (-) Has use of only one hand. (-) Reads, counts, adds and subtracts. (+) (Requires reading prescription glasses has a cane, brace wrist, and glasses, but won't use.) Found other ways to adapt. (+) Understands what money can get for him. (+) Very motivated. (+) Recycles for pay at home. (+)	Worked as a volunteer at the grocery store restocking produce. Had difficulty with bagging candy and other items because he had the use of only one hand. Required assistance to do work. (-) Manager wanted volunteer work only. (-) Classroom teacher's emphasis was volunteer during school day. (-)	Worked at Ambrake-janitorial: cleaned Tables, cleaned windows, dumped ash trays, and cleaned microwaves. Expressed that he hated cleaning. Could not see what he was cleaning. (-) He hated cigarette smoke. (-) Employer fired him, as he required too much assistance. (-)	To explore interests within family, teachers, friends, and other areas. School personnel participated in home visits with Alex and family. (+) Job coach interviewed teachers and other associates to determine Alex's gifts and strengths. (+) (Discovered he liked people who were very friendly and wanted to work a task he could do without assistance and around the public.) (+)	Established a paid Job at Save-Lot-grocery store. (+) Management open minded to carving a job that met his needs. (+) Stocked shelves. (+) Straightened and organized. (+) Carried boxes to the back to be crushed. (+) Always around people. (+) Alex learned to operate the machine to break down empty boxes. (+)

Student	Challenges	Setbacks	Exploration	Outcome
Susan Has Williams Syndrome. Exhibits inappropriate conversation with others. (-) Very sociable (+) Had friends in regular education, they call her often and want to take her to a school dance and other festivities. (+)	Bored with volunteer jobs. Expressed that the jobs were not challenging, no opportunity to have a pay. (+)	Teacher placed in her in volunteer work in kitchen work, laundry, library, & restaurants. She expressed that she hated cleaning. (-) She was terrified of stairs/ step stools. Dependent upon someone to hold her hand on steps. (-)	School personnel participated in home visits with Susan's family. (+) Job coach interviewed her teachers and other associates to determine Susan's gifts and interests. (+) Job coach participated in one-to-one community outings to explore her interests. (+) Susan voiced she wanted more challenging work. (+) Job coach carved work at United Parcel Service, a pilot project. Susan was eager to try several job tasks. (+)	Hired at UPS in picking, uses RF gun. Now she walks up and down ladder (not afraid) carrying RF gun and packages. (+) UPS gave her t shirts, Nike caps, will get her shoes, included in celebrations, (Valentines) and birthdays. (+) Funny Story: She saves her money. She told a story when her dad had to borrow $30.00. She thought that was funny.

Student	Challenges	Setbacks	Exploration	Outcome
Sandy Has cerebral palsy; uses walker at times; confined to a wheel chair. Sandy is 20 years old. Reads at 2nd-grade level (+); performs tasks well from wheel chair. (+) Knows name of money (+), cannot consistently count, limited counting (-); knows next dollar amount. (+) Noted strength: very sociable (+) Talks too much at times. (-) Limitation: Grooming & hygiene skills. (-)	Participated in volunteer job tasks at U.S. Calvary Military store. (+) She liked it, but they weren't interested in hiring. Worked at a discount store placing security tags on items; she didn't enjoy it. (-) The store manager wasn't open to offering frequent support she needed. (-)	She tried a variety of job task experiences, sorting at military store. (-)	School personnel participated in home visits with Sandy's family. (+) Job coach interviewed teachers and other associates to determine Sandy's gifts and interests. (-) Job coach participated in one-to-one community outings to explore her interests. (+) Sandy voiced wanted work where she could use her gift in being friendly to customers along with work tasks she could manage by herself. (+) She wanted to be around people, not working off alone in a corner. (+)	Established a paid job for her at a grocery store. Her work tasks include loading fruits and vegetables on a tray and placing juices into a bag with ties. (+) This job worked well because she can work right from her wheel chair. (+) She collects items from shelves placed by customers and moves them to the appropriate area. (+) Her pleasant mannerism is an asset when helping customers. (+) Coworkers are friendly and open to provide any support she needs. (+)

Student	Challenges	Setbacks	Exploration	Outcome
Neil Has a developmental disability and is confined to a wheel chair. He was runner-up as Home Coming King. (+) Won the Christa McAuliffe Award. (+) Won two awards Frankfort, KY. Highly sociable and very popular. (+) Strong interest in computers and types well. (+)	Very limited, no family support. (-) He looks nice, but has limitations in self care in hygiene. (-)	Worked as a volunteer at Houchens Grocery produce dept. (+) Wheel chair was limiting; could not reach all of display areas. (-) Christmas time – bagged candy and weighed, labeled (+) Store went out of business. (-) Tried training for filing as an office assistant but didn't work; 2nd letter became confusing. (-)	Job coach looked for settings where he could communicate with others and work from wheel chair. (+) Sought desk job. (+) Job developed at Fort Knox Credit Union. (+) (Job coach gave a talk at the Rotary Club) A RC member offered assistance and hired Neil at the Credit Union. (+)	Neil received a paid Job at Fort Knox Credit Union. (+) Does data entry into computer. (+) He earned minimum wage. (+) The employees love him. He also does all the shredding and stuffs envelops. (+)

Student	Challenges	Setbacks	Exploration	Outcome
Devon Is very high functioning, with a mild developmental disability. (+) He is motivated to work. (+) Can assemble furniture and bikes well. (+) Has license and can drive car. (+)	Lacks family support. (-) Had transportation issues when car broke down. (-)	Got married/then divorced. (-) Health problems (in hospital). (-) School attendance was poor. (-)	Job coach talked with teachers and the student. (+) Devon expressed he liked food service (familiar with this work). (+) Moved in with his grandma. (+)	Job coach carved paid job at Shoneys. (+) Works 40 hours a week. (+) Was capable of going on second interview and completing paper work along with orientation with out support from job coach. (+)

Student	Challenges	Setbacks	Exploration	Outcome
Jeremy Is developmentally delayed. Dad is supportive and encourages him to try (+) Is motivated around males. (+) Likes basketball talk and joking around, being part of a group. (+)	Poor motivation. (-) Mom said she has stopped making him be responsible at home. It is easier to do work for him than to argue with him. (-)	Agreed to try some job tasks in fast food and school cafeteria. (+) He expressed that he hated food service work. (-)	School personnel did home visits. (+) Job coach interviewed teachers. (+) Job coach participated on community outings with Jeremy in a small group. (+) Is motivated around males. (+) Likes basketball talk and joking around, being part of a group. (+) Expressed that he did not want a job coach with him, embarrassed. (+) He needed coworkers with positive attitudes toward work.	Obtained paid job at K mart. (+) Unloaded truck with other coworkers. (+) Worked 15 hours a week. (+)

Student	Challenges	Setbacks	Exploration	Outcome
Kristin Has Down syndrome and is developmentally disabled. Has some reading knowledge on a repetitive community word list. (+) Good with numbers, basic adding and subtracting. (+) Loves music. (+) Very sociable, friendly, light hearted and agreeable. (+) No transportation issues to get to work. (+)	Clingy and dependent. (-)	She fears riding a school bus to work without job coach. (-) Overcame it after several attempts. (+) Strong family support. (+)	School personnel participated in home visits with Sandy's family. (+) Job coach interviewed teachers and other associates to determine Sandy's gifts and interests. (+) Job coach participated in one-to-one community outings to explore her interests. (+) She likes to work around people she could talk and help them do their job. (+)	Job coach searched a variety of jobs, but found Subway to be the most ideal. (+) Kristin has a paid job working in the drive-through and assists others in making sandwiches. (+) Restocks chips, lids, cups and keeps ice machine filled. (+) Likes job. (+)

Student	Challenges	Setbacks	Exploration	Outcome
Fred Has a mild developmental disability and an emotional behavioral disability. He attended an alternative school. Always shows respect and exhibits good manners. (+) Reads at 6th-grade level. (+) Understands money and is motivated to work for it. (+) Is quiet and shy.	Manager at UPS where Fred has a job says he lacks motivation. Sits down on job. (-) Takes extra bathroom breaks. (-) States that his leg hurts.	Hours were cut from 1-5, 5 days a week to 9 to 11 am, 2 days a week. (-) Managers suggested this schedule reduction because of his lack of motivation. They provided more support and were encouraged with results of his behavior. (+)	Fred expressed he wanted to work; liked UPS. Mother worked at factory next door and wanted the job to work out for him. Job works well for family because he has transportation to UPS.	Has paid job — UPS. Fred attends school all day and works from 1:00 to 5:00 pm. 5 days a week. This worked well for several months. (+) Fred was eventually terminated. (-) Job coach surprised because everything was going so well. UPS stated they saw a lack of motivation. (-)

Student	Challenges	Setbacks	Exploration	Outcome
Cynthia Has autism and a developmental disability. Works well with repetitive tasks. (+) Reads at 6th-grade level. (+) Plays the piano extremely well. Plays by hearing the songs. (+) Likes data entry and types well on computer. (+)	Yells out when she is confused. She also exhibits echolalia.	Participated in work tasks in office settings as a volunteer. (+) There was no option for pay. (-) Participated at UPS in packing. (+) It didn't work well; too many steps on the job. (-)	School personnel participated in home visits with Cynthia's family. (+) Job coach interviewed teachers and other associates to determine her gifts and interests. (+) Job coach participated in one-to-one community outings and class field trips to observe her interests. (+)	Job coach carved a paid job at a local newspaper. (+) Coworkers supportive. (+) She retyped old articles lost in the archives; data entry.

Individual	Challenges	Setbacks	Exploration	Outcome
Trent Has autism. He works well with repetitive work tasks that he can see through to the completion. (+) Trent loves all kinds of music. (+) He enjoyed helping his grandmother with yard work. (+) He likes to walk his dog. (+) Trent enjoys walking on the treadmill at the YMCA. (+)	Has good and bad days. Needed support for transportation. Requires coworker support while working. Needs redirection when becoming agitated.	Trent had a number of job experiences: Biggs Dept. Store, Value Market Grocery Store, YMCA, and Papa Johns Pizza. (+) He was fired from the YMCA and Papa John's Pizza. (-) He worked at the YMCA; gathered towels in men's locker room and laundered and folded towels. (+) Trent was fired from job because he became upset when a coworker gave him another task the last 15 minutes of his shift. (-) Had a job at Papa John's folding pizza boxes, but was fired when he obsessed on arranging the jars and cans on the shelf. It interfered with his work. (-)	Trent had several person-centered-planning meetings. (+) The team determined that he enjoyed working at Value Market. There he bagged candy and placed produce items for on display. (+) He left his job because his family moved to another part of town. (-) After he began living independently, the employment specialist negotiated a job whereby Trent and his live in support, Jason were hired as a team. (+)	The employment provider and the employment specialist observed the jobs tasks at a retail store. (+) Out of several, they determined that Trent could place security tags on items. (+) He had a job for one year working 8 hours a week. (+)

Individual	Challenges	Setbacks	Exploration	Outcome
Trent (continued) Trent lost his job after one year of working at Kmart as it downsized. (-) Trent's coping skills were notably stronger. (+)	Trent still has good and bad days. (+) His days are not all bad. Continues to need support for transportation to and from work and around the community. Jason, his live-in, provides that assistance. (+) Trent continues to need natural support from coworkers while working and when agitated, needs redirection.	There are very few setbacks at present time. (+) Trent struggled with obsessions the first 8 months living independently, but overcame many of them with support from live-in roommate. (+)	Trent had several person-centered-planning meetings. (+) Trent's mom contacted a cousin in Michigan, who was a store manager of Meijer. (+) The cousin then contacted store managers in Louisville to arrange an interview for Trent. (+) His mom showed a video of Trent working on his last job at K-mart. (+) The employment provider and Trent 's mom requested that Trent and Jason be hired as a team, just as they were at Kmart. (+)	Trent and Jason were hired as a team to work in the lawn and garden. (+) They were employed for 8 hours per week the first 6 months. (+) One year later they were employed 12 hours a week and Trent had an additional job description, cleaning out the pet cages. (+) During the second year, Trent was working up to 20 hours a week. (+) No longer needing support from Jason who was hired with him as a team. (+) Five years after working at Meijers, Trent has been in charge of the Pet Department. (+)

Hosting a Transition Fair

How to Host a Districtwide Transition Fair

One option of providing transition information to students and parents/advocates is to host a district wide transition fair. Some have named it a resource fair. In the school district where I consulted, we hosted several transition fairs. During the second year, we collaborated with an independent school district to host a transition fair and drew nearly 400 people. Some of the benefits that came out of each fair include:

- Students and families received information about a variety of options about college and training program options from exhibitors.

- Families received information about particular state agencies, services, and resources and were able to direct questions on site to the agency representatives.

- One outcome resulted in a pilot project with the Department of Vocational Reha-bilitation, the school system, and United Parcel Service to employ eligible students with special needs. (This is currently a rare opportunity, but it represents the type of endeavor that could result in hundreds of job opportunities in community after community. What is required is the willingness for different private companies and public agencies to work together, utilizing the ingenuity that resides in every lo-cale.)

- The community at large obtained information about community services that all can access and participated in a fun event that offered participants a chance to win door prizes and listen to a variety of informative speakers.

Steps in Planning a Transition Fair

Meet with the special ed director to establish a calendar date for fair. Have it entered in the district calendar.

Set up a committee to design the brochure and transition fair logo.

Arrange with administrators and other school personnel a focused effort to:

- recruit volunteer teachers for the transition fair.

- request that all special education teachers attend the fair.

- actively promote the transition fair at all IEP meetings and to all students.

Set a meeting date to brainstorm who to invite and what the transition fair will offer. En-courage all school personnel who are interested to come. We chose to blend fun with work so we met at a restaurant. Discuss various information:

- Decide on a theme for the fair.

- Determine where to hold the fair.

- Make a list of all schools/agencies to invite. We decided to have interactive booths such as self-evaluation for learning styles and a test of one's skill at rock climbing. Also invited representatives from the National Guard. These ideas drew broad in-terest.

- Draft an invitational letter and send to the school/agency.

- Follow-up with phone calls to inquire about their interest.

- Determine room availability to hold presentations.

- Make handout noting name of presenter, room #, topic, and time presenting.

- One month prior to fair, make phone calls to ensure their attendance.

Committees

Sign Committee (make a sign for each booth)

Name Tag Committee (with transition fair logo)

Advertising Committee (radio stations and newspaper)

Refreshment committee (We served cookies and punch. Each school placed an order for a certain number of cookies a few days prior to the fair.)

Speaker Recruitment Committee

Donation Prize Committee

Equipment Committee

Volunteer Committee for the night of the fair. Tasks included:

- Visitor sign in sheet.

- Passing out handouts with name of each booth/agency/school.

- Pass out evaluation form.

- Pass out tickets for door prizes.

- Volunteer to call out winners.

- Volunteer to gather and arrange door prizes on table.

- Volunteer as a hostess, helping families find what they need.

The community at large participated in a fun event that promoted awareness of the capabilities and contributions that persons with disabilities can make.

Sample Memo to Parents:

"Eighty percent of success is just showing up."

Why Should You Want to Attend Hardin County and Elizabethtown Transition Fair?
The fair offers comprehensive information about the services by numerous community agencies, regional universities/training programs, and developmental services and resources. We encourage all members in the community, surrounding counties, families, and all students with special needs to attend. Over 400 attended in 2003. Mark your calendars now for 2004.

What You Will Find at "Community Unity"
- Meet new people who can answer your questions about your future.

- Receive important information from agencies and schools.

- Take a fun, quick career inventory, among other interactive activities.

- Watch a video on the transition to adult life produced by the IHDI at University of Kentucky.

- Enjoy cookies and punch.

- WIN DOOR PRIZES!!!!!!

Come and Hear Expert Speakers on These Topics:
- UPS of Elizabethtown, KY — Gerald Bickel will be speaking about what this innovative company is doing to hire persons with disabilities, focusing on a pilot project involving UPS, Hardin County Schools, and Dept. of Vocational Rehabilitation.

- Trusts and Estate Planning — Greg Simpson and Clyde Lang present financial planning for the future for an individual with developmental disabilities.

- SSI/SSDI — Tim Sloan talks about program benefits. You can have a job and still keep SSI benefits.

- Supports for Community Living (A Medicaid funded program) — Debra Hall presents on living in your own place. Find out about these community resources.

Exhibit Booth List
- University of Louisville
- Carl Perkins Rehabilitation Center
- Sullivan University
- Morehead State University
- Western Kentucky University
- Murray State University
- Elizabethtown Beauty
- Elizabethtown Community College
- McKendree College
- Spencerian College
- ITT Technical School
- Eastern Kentucky University
- Department of Vocational Rehabilitation
- Independence Bound
- Louisville Technical Institute
- Adult Education of Hardin County Schools
- Supports for Community Living
- RETS (Tech School in Louisville)
- Cedar Lake Lodge
- Almost Family
- Department of Employment Services
- Commission for Special Heath Needs
- Supported Living
- Hardin Memorial Hospital
- Supported Employment
- 4 C's
- Kentucky Autism Training Center
- First Steps
- ADECCO Employment
- Kentucky National Guard
- US Navy Recruiting
- Hardin County Young Democrats
- Hardin County Young Republicans
- Center for Accessible Living
- River Region Cooperative
- Community-Based Work Transition Program
- Manpower Employment
- Communicare (local comprehensive care center)
- Association for Retarded and Handicapped Citizens
- Youth Services Center/Hardin County School
- TACK

Appendix G

Resources

Listed below are some of the major governmental resources that you should know about while seeking and accessing assistance for the young adult with a developmental disability. You can inquire about your eligibility or your young adult's eligibility for these programs. I strongly recommend applying for a Supported Living Grant. Funds are scarce but don't let that stop you. Policymakers need to be aware of our needs, and by applying for the grant you are not only actively empowering yourself, but also increasing awareness of the shortage of resources to met existing needs.

Supported Living Grants

Contact your state disability agency and inquire about a Supported Living Grant. Trent has one. Without it, I would not have had the funds to hire a community coach and then later Jason, his live-in assistant. Supported Living can swing doors wide open for a person with a disability, helping him/her purchase the necessary supports to interact and participate within the community. A mother once expressed in simplest terms what she wanted for her son after graduation. "I want him to have a life. That means money, friends, and a job that has some dignity and worth, instead of just sitting around."

Helping a young adult carve out a future is often confusing and difficult. It's like being on a scavenger hunt searching for treasures. Only it isn't a game or pretend play. It is real.

Family members, teachers, and friends can help the person find the treasures to living in the community. The discovery process involves gathering previous experiences and searching through them. Notice the gems — they are the person's desires, abilities and gifts. If we listen to their stories, they will show us their jewels. "Personalization" is the success of the Supported Living program.

Here are just some situations that a Supported Living Grant could fund to help the individual access the community and enjoy increased independence.

1. a person to escort the individual to various activities, shopping, eating out in restaurants, bowling, movies, plays, and other community events.
2. negotiating additional supports by coworkers on the job.
3. equipment to assist with mobility or increase communication.
4. an expert knowledgeable in facilitating the individual's person-centered-planning meetings, or in providing valuable information about guardianship and setting up trusts.
5. respite for the individual so family members can participate in major life events such as weddings, enjoy friendships, hobbies, or spend individual time with siblings/spouse.
6. art therapy.
7. a roommate or live-in assistant to help the individual live independently in his/her own home.

The Supported Living Grant is intended to help connect a person with a disability to events, activities, and situations, to enable him/her to interact within various community environments. To design a plan that is specifically tailored for the individual is the goal. It is important to note that it is *not* intended to fund any program/service that places persons with disabilities solely with other persons having disabilities. For instance, the program will not fund a day habilitation program or other separate services.

All persons with disabilities are vital, living souls who have potential for growth and giving. But they may need help through the process of exploration and discovery, which requires planning and effort. The treasures we find turn into values, which offer new perspectives on life. But it does more than that; it also offers persons a chance to know who they can become and what they can offer. That is what Supported Living did for my son and is doing for others.

Not all states have this particular grant. However, if you want to find out more about a Supported Living Grant and you live in Kentucky, contact the regional comprehensive care center in your area or call 1-800-372-2973; TTY 1-800-627-4702.

Social Security Insurance (SSI)

SSI is a program that is based on financial need. You can qualify if you are over 65, blind or disabled. SSI is designed to provide a minimum income to people unable to work due to disability or retirement, who are otherwise uninsured or underinsured, and have insufficient income from other sources.

Families often believe that when their child gets a job, he will lose his SSI check. That is not true. When a young adult who is receiving SSI gets a paid job, his check will decrease. But when combining the wages he earns per month with his job and the reduced check, he will make more money than before when he did not have a job and drew the SSI check only.

You can apply by making an appointment at the local Social Security office or calling 1-800-772-1213, TTY number 1-800-325-0778, or by visiting the web site at http://www.ssa.gov

Social Security Disability Insurance (SSDI)

SSDI is a federal cash benefit that may be available if a person is disabled. SSDI eligibility is determined depending on having a disability and on prior work. A spouse and other dependents might be eligible for SSDI based on work history.

You can apply by making an appointment at the Social Security office or calling 1-800-772-1213, TTY number 1-800-325-0778, or by visiting the web site at http://www.ssa.gov

Supports for Community Living (SCL)

SCL (in Kentucky) is a Medicaid-funded program. States have various names for this program.

Basically the program provides services to individuals with disabilities, enabling them to live in the home or in the community rather than in an institution. SCL services include the following: support coordination, residential supports, community habilitation, supported employment, behavior supports, psychological services, occupational therapy, physical therapy, speech therapy, respite care, and specialized medical equipment and supplies. You qualify if you have mental retardation or a developmental disability. You must meet Medicaid requirements. There is a long waiting list for this service. If you live in Kentucky, you can get an application by caling 1-800-372-2973 or TTY 1-800-627-4702. For individuals resideing outside of Kentucky, contact your state's Medicaid Waiver Program for further information.

Department of Vocational Rehabilitation (DVR)

DVR offers a wide range of services to individuals with disabilities to prepare, secure, and maintain a job. It can also offer services when a person becomes unemployed. Persons who have a physical or mental disability, or receive Social Security disability benefits, qualify. Each state has this agency, however, the names are different. Contact the regional comprehensive care center in your area for information about Vocational Rehabilitation services or call 1-800-637-5627.

State Emergency Funds

These are funds that are offered through your community mental health and developmental regional program or nonprofit agency. They are based upon emergency cases and need. Contact the regional comprehensive care center in your area for information.

Supported Employment

This service assists persons with severe disabilities to find and maintain employment in an integrated setting with long-term support.

Persons who receive Supplemental Security Insurance qualify. However, it is not necessary to receive SSI to qualify. Persons who have a severe mental or physical disability can apply for this service. Also, if a disability has interfered with getting and/or keeping a job, a person may be eligible. Apply for Supported Employment at the Department of Vocational Rehabilitation. Contact the regional comprehensive care center in your area and ask about Vocational Rehabilitation services and provider agencies.

Other Resources for Learning About Inclusion

Alliance for Technology Access
800-455-7970; 415-455-4575 (Voice)
415-455-0491 (TTY)
E-mail: atainfo@ataccess.org
Website: www.ataccess.org

American Council of the Blind
800-424-8666; 202-467-5081
E-mail: ncrabb@erols.com
Website: www.acb.org

American Council on Rural Special Education (ACRES)
785-532-2737
E-mail: acres@ksu.edu
Website: www.ksu.edu/acres

American Foundation for the Blind (AFB)
800-232-5463 (Voice)
212-502-7662 (TTY)
Publications available in Spanish
E-mail: afbinfo@afb.org
Website: www.afb.org

American Occupational Therapy Association (AOTA)
301-652-2682 (Voice)
Website: www.aota.org

American Physical Therapy Association (APTA)
800-999-2782; 703-684-2782 (Voice)
703-683-6748 (TTY)
E-mail: practice@apta.org
Website: www.apta.org

American Speech-Language-Hearing Association (ASHA)
800-498-2071 (V/TTY)
301-571-0457 (TTY)
Publications available in Spanish; Spanish speaker on staff
E-mail: actioncenter@asha.org
Website: www.asha.org

American Therapeutic Recreation Association
703-683-9420
E-mail: atra@atra-tr.org
Website: www.atra-tr.org

Angelman Syndrome Foundation
800-432-6435; 630-734-9267
E-mail: asf@adminsys.com
Website: www.angelman.org

Anxiety Disorders Association of America
301-231-9350
E-mail: AnxDis@adaa.org
Website: www.adaa.org

Aplastic Anemia & MDS International Foundation
800-747-2820; 410-867-0242
E-mail: aamdsoffice@aol.com
Website: www.aamds.org

The Arc (formerly the Association for Retarded Citizens of the U.S.)
301-565-3842
E-mail: Info@thearc.org
Website: www.thearc.org

Asperger Syndrome Education Network (ASPEN®)
732-321-0880
E-mail: info@aspennj.org
Website www.aspennj.org

Association for Professionals in Supported Employment
804-278-9187
Website: www.apse.org/

Attention Deficit Disorders Associations – Southern Region
281-897-0982
E-mail: oflanigan@adda-sr.org
Website: www.adda-sr.org/

Autism One
Website: www.autismone.org

Autism Society of America
800-328-8476; 301-657-0881
Publications available in Spanish
Website: www.autism-society.org

Beach Center on Disability
785-864-7600
Website: www.beachcenter@ku.edu

Brain Injury Association (formerly the National Head Injury Foundation)
800-444-6443; 703-236-6000
Publications available in Spanish
E-mail: FamilyHelpline@biausa.org
Website: www.biausa.org

Capacity Works
888-840-8578
Website: www.capacityworks.com

Center for Mental Health Services, Knowledge Exchange Network
Publications available in Spanish
800-789-2647 (Voice)
301-443-9006 (TTY)
E-mail: ken@mentalhealth.org
Website: www.mentalhealth.org

Childhood Apraxia of Speech Association
412-343-7102
E-mail: helpdesk@apraxia-kids.org
Website: http://www.apraxia-kids.org

Children and Adults with Attention-Deficit/Hyperactivity Disorder (CHADD)
800-233-4050
E-mail: national@chadd.org
Website: www.chadd.org

Children with Disabilities
E-mail: ChildrenDisabilities@ncjrs.org
Website: www.childrenwithdisabilities.ncjrs.org/

Council for Exceptional Children (CEC)
703-620-3660 (Voice)
703-264-9446 (TTY)
E-mail: cec@cec.sped.org
Website: www.cec.sped.org/

DAC (disabled Action committee)
703-878-1737
E-mail: DAC4VA@aol.com
Web: http://members.aol.com/DAC4VA/index.html

Disability and Business Technical Assistance Centers (DBTACs)
800-949-4232
Website: www.adata.org/dbtac.html

DisAbility.gov
800-FED-INFO
E-mail: webmaster@disability.gov
Website: www.disability.gov/CSS/

Easter Seals-National Office
800-221-6827; 312-726-6200 (Voice)
312-726-4258 (TTY)
E-Mail: info@easter-seals.org
Website: www.easter-seals.org

EMPOWER Colorado
866-213-4631
E-mail: info@empowercolorado.com
Website: www.empowercolorado.com

Families for Early Autism Treatment
916-491-1033
E-mail: webmaster@feat.org
Website: www.feat.org

Families For Hands and Voices
303-300-9763
866-422-0422
E-mail: parentadvocate@handsandvoices.org
Website: www.handsandvoices.org

Family Village
Website: www.familyvillage.wisc.edu/

Family Voices
888-835-5669; 505-867-2368
E-mail: kidshealth@familyvoices.org
Website:www.familyvoices.org

Father's Network
425-747-4004, ext. 218
E-mail: jmay@fathersnetwork.org
Website: www.fathersnetwork.org

Federation of Families for Children's Mental Health
703-684-7710
Publications available in Spanish
E-mail: ffcmh@ffcmh.com
Website: www.ffcmh.org

Inclusion Press International & The Marsha Forest Centre
416-658-5363
Website: www.inclusionpress@inclusion.com

Independent Living Research Utilization Project
713-520-0232
E-mail: ilru@ilru.org
Website: www.ilru.org

Institute on Independent Living
E-mail: admin@independentliving.org
Website: http://www.independentliving.org/

International Resource Center for Down Syndrome
216-621-5858
800-899-3039 (toll-free in OH only)
E-mail: hf854@cleveland.freenet.edu

Learning Disabilities Association of America (LDA)
888-300-6710; 412-341-1515; 412-341-8077
Publications available in Spanish
E-mail: vldanatl@usaor.ne
Website: www.ldanatl.org

National Alliance for the Mentally Ill (NAMI)
800-950-6264; 703-524-7600 (Voice)
703-516-7991 (TTY)
Publications available in Spanish
E-mail: namiofc@aol.com
Website: www.nami.org

National Association of Private Schools for Exceptional Children (NAPSEC)
202-408-3338
E-mail: napsec@aol.com
Website: www.napsec.com

National Attention Deficit Disorder Association
E-mail: mail@add.org
Website: www.add.org

National Autism Association
877-622-2884
Website: www.nationalautismassociation.org/mission..php

National Center for Learning Disabilities (NCLD)
212-545-7510; 888-575-7373
Website: www.ncld.org

National Council on Independent Living
703-525-3406; 703-525-4153 (TTY)
E-mail: ncil@ncil.org
Website: www.ncil.org

National Cued Speech Association (NCSA)
800-459-3529 (TTY)
E-mail: CuedSpDisc@aol.com
Website: www.cuedspeech.org

National Down Syndrome Congress
800-232-6372; 770-604-9500
Spanish speaker on staff
E-mail: NDSCcenter@aol.com
Website: www.ndsccenter.org

National Down Syndrome Society
800-221-4602; 212-460-9330
E-mail: info@ndss.org
Website: www.ndss.org

National Library Service for the Blind &
Physically Handicapped
800-424-8567; 202-707-5100 (Voice)
Publications available in Spanish
E-Mail: nls@loc.gov
Website: www.loc.gov/nls

National Mental Health Association
800-969-6642; 703-684-7722 (Voice)
800-433-5959 (TTY)
Publications available in Spanish
E-mail: nmhainfo@aol.com
Website: www.nmha.org

National Parent Network on Disabilities
202-463-2299 (V/TTY)
E-Mail: npnd@cs.com
Website: www.npnd.org

National Parent to Parent Support and
Information System, Inc.
800-651-1151; 706-374-3822
E-mail: nppsis@ellijay.com
Website: www.nppsis.org

Ontario Adult Autism Research and Support
Network
Website: www.ont-autism.uoguelph.ca/
newpage4.shtml

Obsessive Compulsive Foundation, Inc.
203-315-2190
E-mail: info@ocfoundation.org
Website: www.ocfoundation.org

Oregon Parents United
541-389-0004
Website: www.oregonparentsunited.org
E-mail: OPU@peak.org

Parents Helping Parents: Parent-Directed
Family Resource Center for Children
with Special Needs
408-727-5775
Publications available in Spanish; Spanish
speaker on staff
E-mail: info@php.com
Website: www.php.com

Prader-Willi Syndrome Association
800-926-4797; 941-312-0400
E-mail: pwsausa@aol.com
Website: www.pwsausa.org

President's Committee's Job Accommodation
Network
800-526-7234 (Voice/TTY)
E-mail: jan@.icdi.wvu.edu
Website: www.jan.wvu.edu

Smart Kids with Learning Disabilities
203-226-6831
E-mail: Info@SmartKidswithLD.org
Web: www.SmartKidswithLD.org

Special Olympics International
202-628-3630
Publications available in Spanish and
French; Spanish & French speaker on staff
E-mail: specialolympics@msn.com
Website: www.specialolympics.org/

TASH
410-828-8274
Website: www.tash.org/

Technical Assistance Alliance for Parent
Centers (the Alliance)
888-248-0822; 952-838-9000
Spanish speaker on staff
E-mail: alliance@taalliance.org
Website: www.taalliance.org

Tourette Syndrome Association
  800-237-0717; 718-224-2999
  E-mail: ts@tsa-usa.org
  Website: http://tsa-usa.org/

Trace Research & Development Center
  608-262-6966 (Voice)
  608-262-5408 (TTY)
  E-mail: info@trace.wisc.edu
  Website: http://trace.wisc.edu/

Uniquely Gifted
  Website: www.uniquelygifted.org

United Cerebral Palsy Association, Inc.
  202-776-0406; 800-872-5827 (Voice)
  202-973-7197 (TTY)
  Publications available in Spanish
  E-Mail: ucpnatl@ucpa.org
  Website: www.ucpa.org

US National Easter Seals
  312-726-6200 (Voice)
  312-726-4258 (TTY)
  800-221-6827 (toll-free)
  Website: www.easter-seals.org/

VCU-RRTC on Supported Employment
  1314 West Main Street
  P.O. Box 842011
  Richmond, VA 23284-2011
  804-828-1851 (Voice)
  804-828-2193 (Fax)
  804-828-2494 (TTY)

Williams Syndrome Association, Inc.
  P.O. Box 297
  Clawson, MI 48017-0297
  248-244-2229 (Voice)
  800-806-1871 (Toll-free voice)
  248-244-2230 (Fax)
  E-mail: info@williams-syndrome.org
  Website: www.williams-syndrome.org

I Would Like to Hear from You

If this workbook has inspired your thinking about people with developmental disabilities and the purposeful life they can live, I would like to hear from you.
What is your story? What is the best lesson you have learned that moved you forward?
We can help each other by sharing our stories.

You can write to me at:

Jackie Marquette, Ph.D.
7514 Warrenton Hill Ct.
Louisville, KY 40291

Or send an email to:
Jackie@themarquettegroup.com

About the Author, Jackie Marquette, Ph.D.

Jackie has over 20 years of experience as a special educator and school consultant, and has published in books, journals, and monthly newsletters. Jackie earned her Ph.D. at the University of Louisville, where her research explored how families guided young adults with autism spectrum disorders (ASD) to live independently. Her research also validated a new assessment tool, the Capability and Independence Scale (CAIS)©, which measures an individual's adaptation level with supports. It is also a protocol for professionals across medical, rehabilitation, and educational fields to evaluate personal growth outcomes.

Jackie created Walking the Path© Seminars based on a model designed for families and professionals to guide youth with ASD and developmental disabilities to develop self-expression through positive attributes and personal talents.

From 2000 to 2004, Jackie supervised and coordinated an innovative transition project that established paid jobs in the community for students with mild and severe disabilities for the Hardin County School District in Kentucky. In 1997-1999, she spearheaded the ACT Project through the Kentucky Autism Training Center, which established employment supports for young adults with ASD.

Her son, Trent, has autism. He is employed at the Meijer department store, has his own art business, Trent's Studio, and has lived independently for six years with "creative supports." He has also received the honor as a Kentucky Juried Artist by the Kentucky Arts Council.

Email: jackie@themarquettegroup.com
Web Site: www.themarquettegroup.com

About the Cover Artist, Trent Altman

I am an expressionistic abstract artist working in acrylics and mixed media collage on canvas. My work displays an emphasis and commitment to the process of art making over and above the product. Experiencing my work makes that abundantly clear. You can sense a freedom of expression, movement, energy, and drive through the multiple methods of applying paint and collage materials that I use. With each piece, I discover, explore, and ultimately, share layers and avenues of moods and emotions. The viewer of my work is encouraged to explore, and perhaps can't help but be drawn into, the wonder of the how, what and why of the process that brought the piece to life. For me this process rises above all else as I make art to nurture my mind, heart and soul, reaching within myself and sharing with others through the process.

I have exhibited my paintings in Long Island, Atlanta, Chicago, Nashville, Dallas, Eureka Springs, AR, and Providence, RI. My art has sold in every state in the United States, as well as in Japan, England, and Canada.

To view my art, go to: www.independencebound.com/trentsprints

Other Books of Interest for Adolescents and Young Adults with Autism Spectrum Disorders and Related Disabilities

Asperger Syndrome and Adolescence: Practical Solutions for School Success

Brenda Smith Myles, Ph.D., and Diane Adreon

Code 9908   Price: $23.95

Asperger Syndrome – An Owner's Manual: What You, Your Parents and Your Teachers Need to Know; An Interactive Guide and Workbook

Ellen S. Heller Korin

Code 9960   Price $17.95

Asperger Syndrome – An Owner's Manual 2: For Older Adolescents and Adults; What You, Your Parents and Friends, and Your Employer, Need to Know

Ellen S. Heller Korin, M.Ed.

Code 9996   Price: $19.95

Developing Talents: Careers for Individuals with Asperger Syndrome and High-Functioning Autism

Temple Grandin with Kate Duffy

Code 9925   Price: $19.95

Ask and Tell: Self-Advocacy and Disclosure for People on the Autism Spectrum

Edited by Stephen M. Shore; foreword by Temple Grandin; contributing authors: Ruth Elaine Hane, Kassiane Sibley, Stephen M. Shore, Roger N. Meyer, Phil Schwarz, Liane Holliday Willey

Code 9940   Price: $21.95

Life and Love: Positive Strategies for Autistic Adults

Zosia Zaks

Code 9965   Price $24.95

A 5 Is Against the Law! Social Boundaries: Straight Up! An honest guide for teens and young adults

Kari Dunn Buron

Code 9975   Price: $19.95

To order:
Autism Asperger Publishing Co.
P.O. Box 23173
Shawnee Mission, Kansas 66283-0173
www.asperger.net
877-277-8254

APC

Autism Asperger Publishing Co.
P.O. Box 23173
Shawnee Mission, Kansas 66283-0173
www.asperger.net
877-277-8254